Secrets of the Bass Pros

MINNETONKA, MINNESOTA

Talk to leading bass pros like David Fritts, Bill Dance, Rick Clunn and others, and they'll tell you that it's the little things that separate them from other anglers, not a magic lure or bait. This book, Secrets Of The Bass Pros, highlights the techniques of our nation's best bass anglers, including those little things they do that always make such a big difference. Edited by former fisheries biologist turned angling educator, Dick Sternberg, this book is a must for every serious bass angler!

Steve Pennaz

Secrets of the Bass Pros

Dick Sternberg
Editor

Tom Carpenter
Director of Book Development

Dan Kennedy
Book Production Manager

Michele Teigen
Senior Book Development Coordinator

Bill Lindner, Tom Heck, Mike Hehner
Photography

David Schelitzche, Julie Cisler
Designers

9 10 11 12 13/ 05 04 03 02 01

ISBN 0-914697-94-3

North American Fishing Club
12301 Whitewater Drive
Minnetonka, MN 55343
www.fishingclub.com

Contents

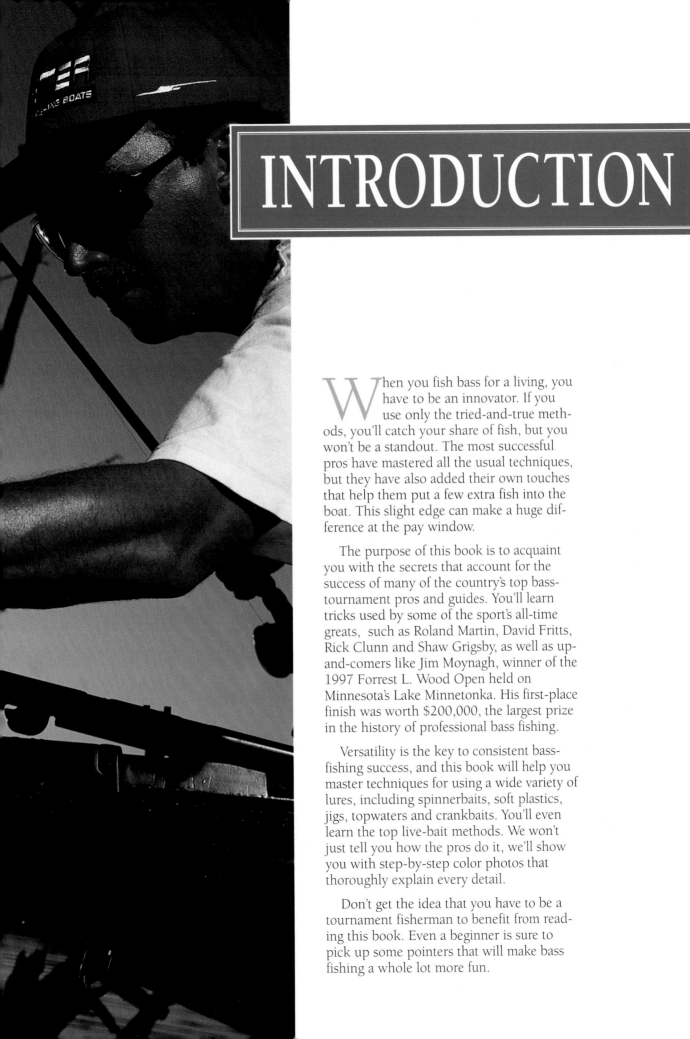

INTRODUCTION

When you fish bass for a living, you have to be an innovator. If you use only the tried-and-true methods, you'll catch your share of fish, but you won't be a standout. The most successful pros have mastered all the usual techniques, but they have also added their own touches that help them put a few extra fish into the boat. This slight edge can make a huge difference at the pay window.

The purpose of this book is to acquaint you with the secrets that account for the success of many of the country's top bass-tournament pros and guides. You'll learn tricks used by some of the sport's all-time greats, such as Roland Martin, David Fritts, Rick Clunn and Shaw Grigsby, as well as up-and-comers like Jim Moynagh, winner of the 1997 Forrest L. Wood Open held on Minnesota's Lake Minnetonka. His first-place finish was worth $200,000, the largest prize in the history of professional bass fishing.

Versatility is the key to consistent bass-fishing success, and this book will help you master techniques for using a wide variety of lures, including spinnerbaits, soft plastics, jigs, topwaters and crankbaits. You'll even learn the top live-bait methods. We won't just tell you how the pros do it, we'll show you with step-by-step color photos that thoroughly explain every detail.

Don't get the idea that you have to be a tournament fisherman to benefit from reading this book. Even a beginner is sure to pick up some pointers that will make bass fishing a whole lot more fun.

CRANKBAITS

Advanced Crankbait Fishing

by Tim Tucker and Mark Hicks

Used to be, the crankbait was considered a "no-brainer" lure, because all you had to do was cast it out and reel it in. That stigma, no doubt, limited the lure's popularity in pro-bass circles.

But when David Fritts used crankbaits to win the prestigious BASS Masters Classic in 1993, the crankbait's popularity suddenly skyrocketed. To further rev up the crankbait craze, Fritts used these big-lipped divers to capture another B.A.S.S. event and a Red Man regional tournament, all within a three-month period.

But Fritts has enjoyed plenty of help when it comes to spreading the gospel of crankbait fishing. Four of the six BASS Masters Classic champions in the 1990s relied heavily on these diving baits. Pros like four-time world champion Rick Clunn and Paul Elias had shown us the fish-catching ability of crankbaits over the years, but it took Fritts – the undisputed guru of these lures – to drive the point home.

All of a sudden, crankbaits are the hot ticket among bass enthusiasts. Crankbaits have won over a legion of followers that stretch from California to Connecticut and Maine to Florida.

The rise in popularity is understandable. Besides the fact that crankbaits produce fish on a consistent basis in every corner of the country, these lures are not discriminating. Novice anglers adore crankbaits because they don't require the deft touch that a plastic worm demands. Simply retrieving a crankbait ignites its built-in, fish-attracting action.

While there is beauty in its simplicity, crankbait fishing has become a real art to dedicated diving-lure fishermen, who have taken the time and effort to learn its intricacies. These knowledgeable anglers have taken crankbaits from their "dummy bait" reputation to an advanced form of angling.

In the hands of a talented fisherman who understands the principles of advanced crankbaiting, these wooden or plastic diving baits are versatile fishing tools. With the proper education and enough practice, it's possible to catch bass in places you could never reach; places you avoided; or places where you never caught fish before.

Crankbaiting Equipment

The proper tackle is of utmost importance in crankbait fishing.

The rod, an often-overlooked instrument among crankbait anglers, is the absolute key to getting the most out of a diving lure. Standard equipment among good crankbait fishermen is a long (7½-foot), stout rod. Some pros prefer flippin' sticks. The long rod accomplishes two things: It allows you to get more depth out of a crankbait by generating a longer cast. It gives you a stronger

David Fritts

David Fritts is a member of professional fishing's millionaire club, having passed the $1 million mark in career earnings on the B.A.S.S. and Forrest L. Wood (FLW) circuits. He has won many B.A.S.S. tournaments, the coveted B.A.S.S. Angler of the Year award, the prestigious BASS Masters Classic and two FLW tour events.

Fritts makes his home in Lexington, North Carolina.

A long, powerful rod is a must in crankbaiting.

hook set, especially when you have a lot of line out after making a lengthy cast.

Until recent years, few anglers ever gave much thought to the composition of the rod they used for crankbaiting. Most anglers were caught up in the graphite craze of the past decade, charmed by the sensitivity and feather-light weight of those rods.

Then Texan Rick Clunn broke all the BASS Masters Classic records by crankbaiting 75 pounds of bass in three days to run away with the 1986 title using an old fiberglass rod he had found buried in the back of the Daiwa catalog. That took the lid off a secret he had maintained for years. Graphite rods can cause even the most seasoned fishermen to consistently lose fish when using fast-moving lures like crankbaits.

"Through years of fishing both graphite and fiberglass rods, I am convinced that the

action and sensitivity of graphite rods work against hooking fish well on fast-moving baits," Clunn explains. "And the better a fisherman you are, the more it will hurt you.

"What happens with graphite is that those rods are so super-sensitive that we're reacting a split-second faster than we had been able to react before. And the fish is just not getting the lure into his mouth far enough and long enough before the rod and the fisherman feels him and reacts. We're talking about split-seconds, but that's the amount of time that's going to determine whether the bass is hooked deep or it's hooked on the outside and is able to spit the lure out."

The reel is also an important consideration in crankbait fishing. In recent years, reel manufacturers have made tremendous strides in increasing the take-up speed of their products. Ten years ago, the fastest gear-ratio found on a baitcasting reel was 3.7

to 1. Today, 5-to-1 ratio reels are common-place and high-speed, 6.2-to-1-ratio models are available.

But don't get the idea that faster means better when it comes to crankbait fishing. Veteran diving-lure anglers emphasize that more speed does not necessarily translate into more depth, which seems to be the aim of most crankbait enthusiasts.

"The development of high-speed reels has changed the game and a lot of fishermen haven't adjusted to it," says Paul Elias, a former Classic champion from Mississippi. "First of all, you can actually reel too fast and rob a lure of some of its depth. You can easily over-crank it.

"The biggest problem, though, is that fishermen everywhere have bought these new high-speed reels to replace their older, slower ones. Then they tie on a crankbait, head out to the lake and proceed to crank at the same speed they were accustomed to with the older, slower reel. They don't make a mental adjustment to the fact that they are using a reel that is moving that lure about twice as fast as the old reel did and slow down.

"Two things happen when you over-crank a lure. First, you change the action of the lure. Secondly, it won't run at the same depth. You may have a bait that will run to 12 feet with a moderate retrieve, but if you speed it up, it may only run 10 feet. The common thought among many weekend fishermen, that you get more depth the faster you crank, is one of the biggest fallacies in bass fishing."

A high-speed reel increases retrieve speed without wearing you out, but you may over-crank your bait.

Maximizing Crankbait Depth

It was in 1987 that the super-deep-diving crankbait became the craze. In that year, several lure manufacturers introduced crankbaits that could break the 20-foot barrier. Before that, crankbait fishermen had to be content with reaching maybe the 15-foot mark.

This development opened up a new arena for crankbait enthusiasts. But reaching those depths is not a matter of simply casting one of these super divers out and reeling it back in.

The Importance of Line Size
by Bill Dance

Line size plays a very important role in determining the depth that you can obtain with a crankbait. You are simply going to get more depth with lighter line. The reason is that the lighter the line, the smaller the diameter, so there is less friction coming through the water. The heavier the line, the more resistance because there's more friction.

You would be surprised at the difference that 10-pound test line and 20-pound test make. With the average crankbait, you can get a couple of extra feet of depth with 10-pound test and in many situations, an extra 2 feet can be crucial. But when you use line below 10-pound test, you may actually lose a little depth because of line stretch.

Another problem created by using heavier line with crankbaits is the possibility of altering that all-important vibration pattern. Anything that moves through the water vibrates to some degree, and line also makes noise coming through the water. The diameter of heavier line can change the vibration pattern of a crankbait.

Naturally, the smaller the lure, the more critical the problem becomes – both in terms of depth and vibration. Larger lures do not present that much of a problem.

Lee Sisson is a crankbait expert and a genius at getting maximum depth from these deep-diving baits. But then, he should be. As the former lure designer for the Bagley Bait Company, as well as several other companies, Sisson created crankbaits that found their way into the tackle boxes of most American bass fishermen.

"The first thing to get out of your mind is that the harder you crank, the deeper a lure goes," Sisson says, echoing Elias' thoughts. "Once you overcome the buoyancy factor of the lure itself, it will run at its deepest from that point. To accomplish that, it usually just takes a moderate, comfortable retrieve."

Silt kicked up by a crankbait often triggers strikes.

The most critical aspects involved in getting optimum depth from a crankbait are length of cast and line size (p. 9), Sisson says.

Flippin' sticks and long crankbait rods, which allow two-handed casting, are a necessity. "A long cast is crucial because deep crankbait fishing is a game of angles," Sisson explains. "The longer the cast, the longer your crankbait can work at its maximum depth range.

"For example, say you make a 50-foot cast and your goal is getting the bait to reach 20 feet. If you were somehow able to drop that crankbait straight down, it would take almost half of the line you have cast out to reach 20 feet. So you can eliminate that 20 feet of your line. Now you've only got 30 feet for that bait to work its way down to the structure and back up (as it nears the boat) in a single retrieve. So you can see with a 50-foot cast, your crankbait is not going to be at its maximum depth very long."

"Another way you can lose depth with a crankbait is if the bait is not running dead center," Sisson adds. "If it's running even a foot off to the side, that can cost you a couple of feet of depth. It's critical that the lure run straight."

A crankbait that is not tracking true requires tuning. To tune a crankbait, use a pair of needle-nose pliers to slightly bend the eye of the crankbait in the direction in which you want it to run. For example, if the crankbait is running too much to the left, hold the bait with the lip facing you and turn the eye (where the split ring is attached) slightly to the right. "If you see it move, you've probably gone too far," Sisson advises. "You just have to develop a feel for it."

Another trick developed in recent years to increase crankbait depth by a foot or so is commonly called "kneeling and reeling." Elias popularized

this crankbait technique en route to winning the Classic on the Alabama River.

The technique is simple. Using a long rod, the angler kneels in the boat and keeps as much of his rod tip as possible underwater. Not only does this lower rod position allow the lure to run deeper, it eliminates the surface tension that the line must overcome, meaning less friction and more depth.

More is Not Always Better

While most crankbait fishermen seem obsessed with breaking the depth barrier, an angler that limits the use of crankbaits to deep water is cheating himself.

"The guy who heads for deep water and only fishes a crankbait deep and fast should not consider himself much of a crankbait fisherman," says Paul Elias. "A crankbait is a tool like any lure and to get the maximum amount out of that tool, you've got to apply it to many different situations.

"For example, most people don't realize it, but a crankbait can be worked very, very methodically to catch fish on or near the surface. I often use the larger, more buoyant lures as topwater baits. In shallow-water situations, a real effective technique is to jerk the bait down a couple of feet and then release it and allow it to float back to the surface. With the deep-diving baits that have a big lip and are real buoyant, that bait won't hardly leave that spot. It will actually back up as it floats up. So now you have a

"Feel" your way over a submerged treetop using a crankbait. When you feel the lure bump a branch, hesitate to let it float up, then continue reeling until you bump another branch.

lure that you throw into a little hole in the lily pads and work effectively. That jerk and floating motion seems to drive bass wild. And you can keep this lure in the strike zone a lot longer than other types of baits."

A common technique practiced nationwide is known as "bumping the stump." Crankbait experts agree that these diving baits are most effective when kept in contact with some type of structure – a submerged log, standing timber, an underwater ledge or even sparse types of vegetation. The action a

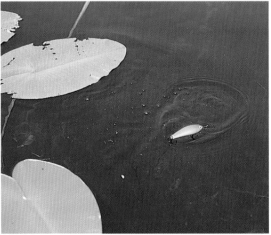

Use a crankbait as a topwater by casting it into a pocket in floating vegetation and giving it a quick pop to make it dive beneath the surface (left). Allow the line to go slack so the bait can float back up: it will actually back up (right), allowing you to pop it again while it remains in the pocket.

crankbait makes when it careens off a log or bounces over a tree limb or pulls away submergent vegetation seems to consistently trigger strikes.

While tournament pros and veteran fishermen understand this technique, the weekend angler is often reluctant to risk his crankbait around some of the densest cover available – the types of places that hold bass.

"Some people will never fish a tree top, because it means using a lure that cost $5 and has a pair of sharp treble hooks on it," Elias says. "They're simply afraid to lose that bait.

"But knowledgeable fishermen will catch a lot of fish off that tree because they know that they can fish it with a crankbait. There's a very simple art to fishing a crankbait in cover like a fallen tree or a tree top. Most deep-diving lures are fairly buoyant, so you use that to your advantage. It's just a matter of cranking the lure down until you feel it bump a limb. Once it hits the limb, if you stop the retrieve, the lure will float above that limb. Then you crank until the lure hits another limb and repeat the procedure. The key is not to be in a big hurry. You can walk a crankbait through some incredibly thick structure."

One could easily argue that the crankbait is the most productive of all bass lures. But only if you take the time to learn the art of advanced crankbaiting can you reap the full benefit of these deep-diving baits.

Crankbait Color Selection
by David Fritts

There is really just a handful of baits that I use almost all the time. In the spring, you should normally stick to browns or crawdad colors, because fish will relate to the rocks and the crawdads are abundant then. Sometimes I throw some chartreuses or maybe a firetiger or a green. A little later in the spring, I'll go to a gray-shad color – something that resembles a shad because the baitfish are really swimming around a lot. It's just a good productive color in late spring when the fish come off the beds.

When it gets hot, I like to throw my green-and-pearls, blue-and-pearls and shad colors. Then a little later, once the skiers get out there and get the water torn up pretty good and it gets a little algae in it, I'll go with my chartreuse-and-greens or chartreuse-and- browns. Then I start going with my toned-down colors like the carp color – the one with the brown shoulders. Just anything a little duller. Blue with chartreuse is a great summer color.

I like the gray-shad in fall. Then I go with my crawdad sometimes, especially if I'm fishing around spotted bass. In the winter, I pretty much stick to a gray-shad, along with some chartreuses and Tennessee-shad. One of the best color patterns put out by Poe has plain white sides with a light-orange belly and a black back. It's a shad color, but it is not a Tennessee-shad. It hasn't got the flash of those other colors. It's a dynamite bait.

David Fritts' Favorite Crankbait Colors

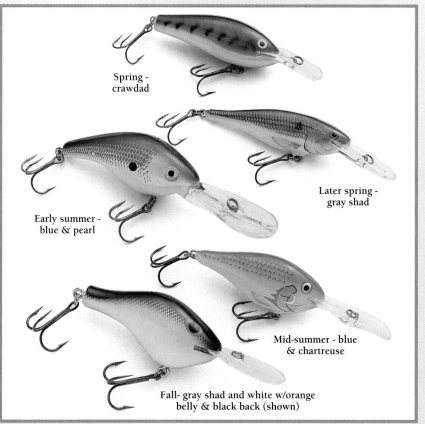

Spring - crawdad

Later spring - gray shad

Early summer - blue & pearl

Mid-summer - blue & chartreuse

Fall- gray shad and white w/orange belly & black back (shown)

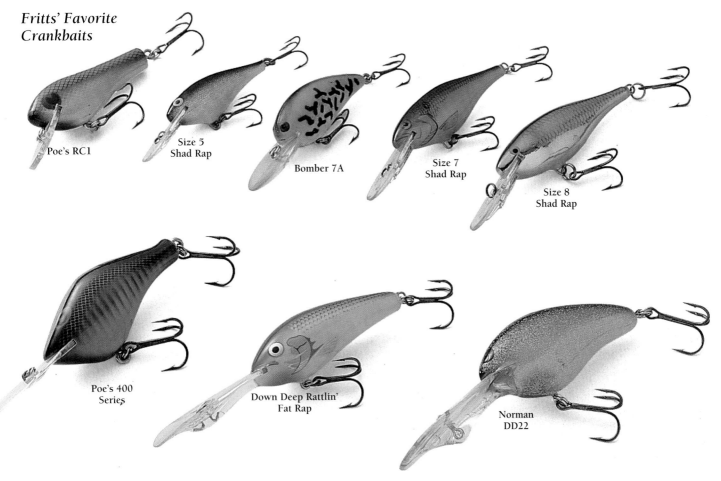

Fritts' Favorite Crankbaits

Poe's RC1

Size 5 Shad Rap

Bomber 7A

Size 7 Shad Rap

Size 8 Shad Rap

Poe's 400 Series

Down Deep Rattlin' Fat Rap

Norman DD22

Selecting Crankbaits

The main consideration in selecting crankbaits is how deep the fish are holding. Serious crankbait anglers carry a selection of shallow-, medium- and deep-running crankbaits.

As a rule, the longer and wider the lip and the straighter the angle at which it extends off the bait's nose, the deeper the bait will dive (right).

Another consideration is body material. Hard plastic baits are the most durable and their hollow body is well suited for internal rattles. Balsa baits are more buoyant, so they work better with a twitching retrieve and are easy to float off of snags, but are much less durable. Cedar baits are intermediate in flotation and durability.

Neutrally buoyant crankbaits are also a good choice, especially when the bass are suspended. A weighted lure runs deep and hangs motionless during pauses, tempting finicky bass to strike. It also may be twitched while hovering in place to provoke bass into action.

Visual Clues for Estimating Running Depth

Lip angle has a major effect on running depth. A bait with lip angle A will run no deeper than 7 feet, while lip angle B may take a bait to 12 feet. A bait with lip angle C may run at a depth of 15 feet or more.

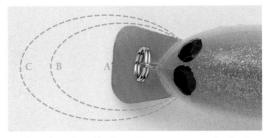

Lip length and width also influence running depth. A bait with a short, narrow lip (A) runs shallowest; one with a long, broad lip, (C) deepest. A bait with an intermediate-shaped lip (B) runs at intermediate depths.

Six Crankbaiting Tips

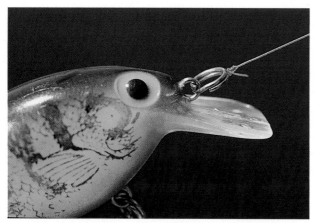

If the crankbait's eye has a split ring, tie on direct, using a clinch knot. Be sure, however, that the knot does not slide into the ring's gap, causing possible line damage and a weak connection.

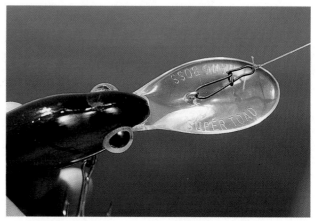

If the crankbait's eye does not have a split ring, connect your line using a loop knot or a light, round-nosed snap (shown). A heavy snap or one with a sharp V will restrict the bait's action.

Cut the leading hook off each one of the bait's trebles when fishing over dense weeds. This reduces fouling, because the hooks most likely to catch weeds are gone.

Once you determine a crankbait's running depth, use a water-proof marker to write the depth on the lure. This way, when you need a lure that runs at a certain depth, you'll know which one to use.

When casting a crankbait into likely fish-holding cover, pause for a few seconds after the bait lands. Curious bass may notice the splash and swim over for a look.

Don't attempt to lip-land a bass hooked on a crankbait; you may wind up with a hook in your hand. Instead, cradle the fish under the belly, as shown.

Crankin' Suspended Bass

by Mark Hicks

A sudden upward swing of the bait often draws strikes.

Almost everything ever written about crankbait fishing ingrains traditional notions that crankbaits must bump stumps, grind bottom, ricochet off rocks and make the contacts and deflections that have long been one of bass fishing's ultimate strike triggers.

While these concepts remain valid, exceptions to the basic rules of bass fishing often result in heavier catches. Cranking for suspended bass qualifies as one of these exceptions.

David Fritts often crankbaits for suspended bass in impoundments. He encounters suspended bass most often during the summer and fall on lakes with fluctuating currents caused by power generating facilities. This is typical of many impoundments throughout the country.

Savvy anglers know that a current encourages bass to move tight to points, humps, ledges and other structures and feed aggressively. Bottom-bouncing crankbait retrieves score well under these conditions.

During periods of slack water, however, bass stop feeding. They may hover 3 or 4 feet above the bottom or roam off the structure in open water. Bass swimming in open water are among the most difficult to catch, but those suspended just above cover remain susceptible to crankbaits.

"They may hold at any depth," says Fritts, "but most of the suspended bass I find are somewhere between 15 and 25 feet deep.

"The most important thing in catching suspended fish," emphasizes Fritts, "is the boat's distance from the bass. When your lure runs through the bass, it should be near the end of the retrieve so it makes a sudden turn upward. That's what triggers the strike.

"If you just run a bait straight through them, you won't catch many. Suspended bass usually aren't actively feeding. That bait has got to change action. When I feel my bait start climbing, I stop it for a second. That's when I get a bite."

Ken Penrod, a successful bass guide from Beltsville, Maryland, spends a good deal of time crankin' for suspended bass on tidewater rivers, like the Potomac.

"I'm convinced," says Penrod, "that anglers will catch more bass – especially on tidal waters – if they back off the bank and retrieve their crankbaits a little farther away from cover than they normally do.

"If you're hitting the shoreline with your crankbaits, you're sitting on top of your fish. I stay well back and make long casts that drop my lures maybe 6 feet from the bank."

This simple presentation runs Penrod's crankbait in front of bass that hold just out from the edges of shoreline cover and drop-offs. Anglers fishing too close to such structures never reach these fish.

Penrod reasons that bass suspend near drop-offs and hold just below the surface current caused by the tide, which he calls a tidal slip.

"The current diminishes the deeper you go," says Penrod. "The fish stage near those drops and move up when they feed. But they're also waiting for opportunities. They know the current is going to bring food to them.

"If you pull a crankbait past them, they'll hit it. It's like walking past someone with a plate of free donuts. Even if you're not hungry, you'll probably grab one."

Giant Plugs For Giant Bass

By Don Wirth

A guy I know once pulled a good stunt at a bass tournament weigh-in. After toting his winning sack of largemouths to the scales, he was asked by the weigh-in official to tell the crowd what lure he'd used to catch his fish. The guy whipped out a 3-foot wooden crankbait with giant treble hooks, a promotional display item he'd borrowed from a local tackle shop. The crowd roared.

But if he were to repeat the stunt at a bass tournament held in California, nobody would laugh. Instead, the crowd would quickly disperse and ransack tackle shops within a hundred-mile radius of the lake in search of 3-foot crankbaits.

On the West Coast these days, monster bass plugs aren't comedic props. The demand for giant plugs – some exceeding a foot in length and priced at more than $50 apiece – is so great that a cottage industry has sprung up to produce them.

Gregg Silks, an avid striper angler from Alta Loma, California, is credited with started the monster-plug craze. "In my quest for a huge striper, I experimented with commercially made striper lures, and I found the bigger the plug I'd use, the bigger the striper I'd catch," he said. "But I realized that to tempt a really monster striper, I needed a different kind of lure – a big, super-erratic bait that captured the panicked look of a fleeing trout or shiner."

Silks was taken by the erratic action of Luhr Jensen's J-Plug, a favorite trolling lure of salmon and trout anglers. "This lure takes darting action to the extreme," he noted. "I carved the same basic sloped-head design. I experimented with both one-piece and jointed bodies. Some of my early designs worked, others didn't."

Eventually Silks came up with a design that gave him the action he was looking for. He named his 15-inch-long creation the Z-Plug.

In experimenting with his homemade plugs, Silks caught bigger stripers to be sure. But once in a while he'd catch a largemouth, too – and it was always a lunker.

"I caught a few 10- to 12-pound largemouths on the Z-Plug," he recalls. "The more I thought about it, the more excited I became about its big-bass potential."

Silks tried to keep his secret weapon under his hat, but word eventually leaked out and copies and spin-offs soon appeared. By 1993, the monster-plug craze was spreading across California's big-bass lakes like wildfire. Giant plugs today are standard equipment for anyone intent on tempting a monster bass from the West Coast's highly pressured lakes.

In the April 1994 American Bass Association tournament on Castaic Lake, Californians Dana Rosen and Darin Tochihara used giant plugs (A.C. Plugs and TNT Lures) to catch six largemouth weighing 63.26 pounds. Three of the six fish weighed more than 12 pounds apiece. The widely publicized catch led to a run on monster plugs on the Coast. Local anglers joked that before long there wouldn't be any table legs left in California.

As word of big-bass catches on these huge baits leaked out, the craze moved across California's borders into Texas and beyond. Today, trophy bass hounds across the country are experimenting with monster plugs.

Opposite: NAFC member Paul Duclos caught what could be a world-record bass on a Castaic Trout Lure.

When & Where
to use Giant Plugs

Casting giant
plugs, which may
weigh more than
a quarter-pound,
requires a long,
stiff rod, such as
a 7½-foot,
heavy-power,
fast-action flip-
pin' stick. Some
plug fishermen
swear by a 7-foot
muskie rod or
even a light surf-
casting rod. Pair
this with a high-
speed baitcaster
(gear ratio of at
least 5:1); giant
plugs require a
fairly rapid
retrieve. Most
anglers prefer
low-vis mono,
from 20- to 30-
pound test, but if
you're trying to
fish deep, use 15-
pound.

Monster plugs are an option in any waters capable of producing largemouth of 10 pounds or more. Although smaller bass will take these big baits, they normally bite better on conventional-size lures.

Giant plugs attract trophy bass for the same reason that magnum soft-plastics do: big bass are lazy; they would rather eat a single large food item than many small ones.

The main reason these huge plugs work so well in California lakes is the lack of dense weedy or brushy cover. The shorelines slope rapidly and the bottoms are usually quite rocky, so there is little chance of the open hooks continually fouling. The fouling problem would most certainly limit the effectiveness of these baits in many of the country's top trophy-bass waters, such as the hydrilla-infested natural lakes of Florida.

Largemouth tend to eat bigger foods during the cold-water months, so that's when you'd expect giant plugs to be most effective. But in California, the normal rules don't apply, because the bass feed heavily on rainbow trout, which are stocked in spring and summer. This explains why California trophy hunters rely on monster plugs year-round.

Giant plugs generally work best when the water is choppy. Not only does the rough water conceal your approach so the fish won't spot you, a choppy surface makes it more difficult for the fish to get a clear look at the bait and detect anything that looks unnatural.

The very best time to try giant plugs is just after a fresh batch of trout have been stocked. The big bass know they've just been offered an easy meal, and they patrol the stocking area for a few days until the trout have dispersed. You know right where to find them and what to throw at them.

Giant Plugs
and How to Fish Them

Over the past few years, several California entrepreneurs have set up basement plug-manufacturing operations to serve the needs of trophy bass hunters. Unfortunately, when their product caught on, few of these manufacturers have been able to keep up with the demand.

Only one, the A.C. Plug (named for its inventor, Allan Cole) was taken on by a major manufacturer (Arbogast) and is widely available.

THE A.C. PLUG. This jointed wooden bait has a soft-plastic shadtail and the basic slant-head design of Luhr Jensen's J-Plug and Gregg Silk's Z-Plug. It is available in 7½, 9½- and 12-inch versions. Although advertised as a surface lure, it will dive up to 5 feet when cast and will run as deep as 15 feet when trolled.

It takes a big mouth to swallow a foot-long plug.

A.C. Plug

Ventura, California, angler, Porter Hall, used a 12-inch A.C. Plug to claim the top prize in Bassin' Magazine's 1995 Big Bass World Championship. His fish, a hulking 18.35-pound largemouth, was taken in 26 feet of water off a main point in Lake Casitas.

"On the day I caught the big fish," Hall said, "I experimented by rigging a 3-ounce banana sinker above the lure to get it down deep. The A.C. Plug is so buoyant, it takes this much weight to sink it. It was the first time I'd ever tried rigging the big lure this way, but it won't be the last." After certifying his catch, Hall released the fish.

Rig a giant plug on a 3- to 6-ounce Gapen Baitwalker for fishing at depths of 25 to 50 feet.

Jack's Whacker

Castaic Trout Lure

Z-Plug

Crankbaits / Giant Plugs for Giant Bass

Jack's Whacker - This bait is manufactured by the Kalin Company of Brawley, California, which is better known for its excellent line of soft-plastic lures. The plug has a jointed body and a plastic tail to give it a serpentine action, much like that of an A.C. Plug. But there are some important differences.

The painting process used in making these lures results in a lifelike finish that appears almost three-dimensional. The head is sloped to make the bait dive deeper than an A.C. Plug, and the soft-plastic tail has a built-in rattle, for extra attraction.

Castaic Trout Lure - Perhaps the most unusual of the California monster plugs is Ken Huddleston's Castaic Trout Lure. This handmade bait has a jointed wooden body, soft-plastic fins and tail and a super-realistic "fish" appearance. It's also the only one of the popular California giants to have a diving lip, albeit a short one.

"The Castaic Trout Lure will run 17 feet deep on 20-pound mono," Huddleston says. "It's designed to mimic trout, which are the primary forage of giant California largemouth, but, depending on color, it can also suggest a big gizzard shad or shiner."

Huddleston claims the lure moves through the water just like a fish. "We spent several weeks at the Fillmore (California) trout hatchery, watching how trout swim, before we designed it. A live trout doesn't move with a big, wide wobble, the way most other monster plugs swim. It moves with a tight wiggle, and that's how our lure swims. In fact, I've cast the lure into newly stocked trout, and they'll swim with it, it's so realistic."

Huddleston says his plug is the only artificial lure legendary California big-bass master Bob Crupi will throw, and many bass over 15 pounds have been taken on it. He's also sold his baits to Texas lunker hunters who fish Lake Fork; they've reported many 10-pound-plus largemouth on them. The lure, available in only an 8½-inch size, is in very short supply. There have been reports of individuals "scalping" them for as much as $100 apiece.

The Z-Plug - "This plug has an erratic action not found in any other lure, store-bought or homemade," says Gregg Silks. "It's also highly versatile. On 20-pound line, it'll crank down to 12 feet or troll to 20 feet. You can pop it on the surface and it blows water, or you can make it plane sideways on top like an injured baitfish. You can troll it on wire or lead-core line, or on a downrigger and get it down to any depth you desire." The Z-Plug is available in a straight and jointed version.

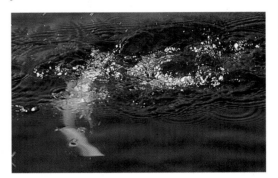

The Z-Plug can be fished like a surface popper.

Two Tips for Fishing Giant Plugs

Work shorelines with many small points. This way, you can cast the plug well past a point and retrieve to make it bump the extension and create an erratic movement that bass can't resist.

Cast to discolored water along a windswept shoreline. Bass feed aggressively in the low-clarity water and aren't as likely to identify the plug as a phony.

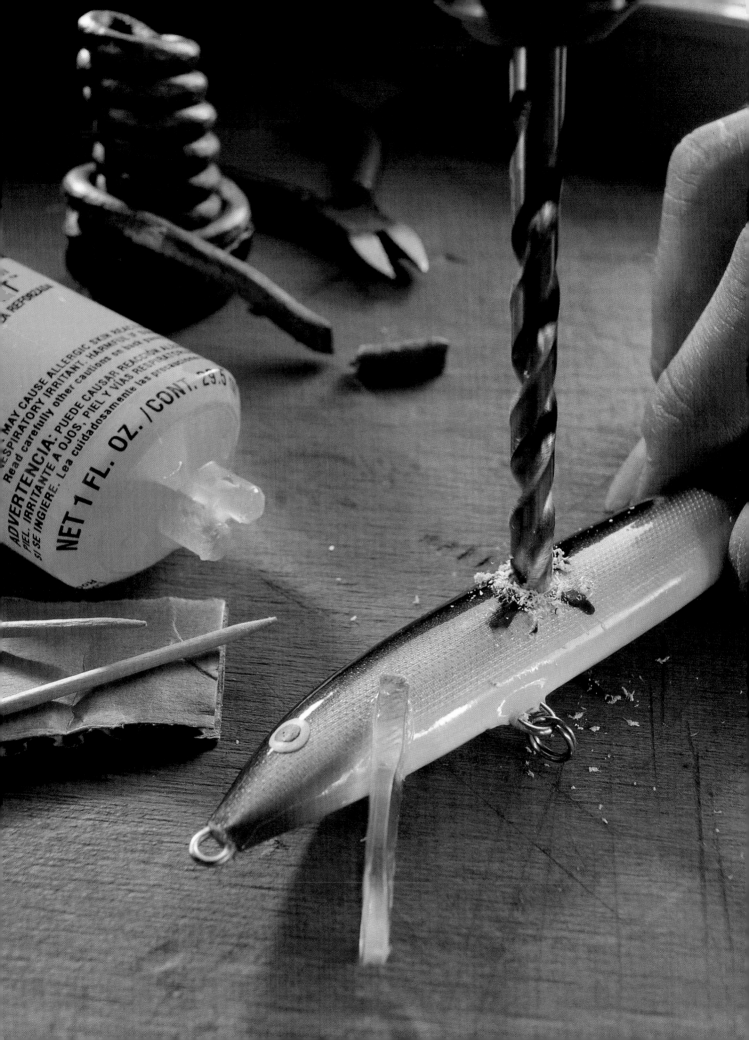

Weighted Jerkbaits
Bass Fishing's Best-Kept Secret?

by Tim Tucker

None of the pros were doing much talking, but some were starting to take notice. Then came a national tournament that blew the lid off of the hand-crafted lure modification that had been shrouded in confidentiality.

The Kentucky BASS Masters Invitational was the coming-out party for the weighted jerkbait.

Held on Kentucky Lake in April of 1992, the tournament destroyed any secrecy associated with hard-plastic jerkbaits that had been hand-weighted for near-neutral buoyancy – giving them the ability to suspend beneath the surface of the water.

Winner Norio Tanabe of Japan, runner-up Mike Saleeba of Ohio and Missouri's Randall Hudson (fourth place) all scored impressively on weighted Smithwick Rattlin' Rogues. And a pair of veteran Texas pros, Rick Clunn (Storm ThunderStick) and Gary Klein (Bomber Long A) finished third and fifth, respectively, on modified jerkbaits.

When the top five finishers in a major tournament use the same, unusual adaptation of a standard lure, the fishing world takes notice.

"The jerkbait was a very confidential bait among the professional fishermen that were in the know," says Rick Clunn.

Clunn has been a fan of the minnow-shaped, shallow-diving lures since his days as a guide on Lake Conroe in the late 1970s. The basic design of the jerkbait gives it an alluring look and action.

"The thing that really makes jerkbaits good is that they catch numbers, as well as quality bass," he says. "I think it's the action of the bait and the size of the bait.

"It has an elongated shape and you can get it down there pretty deep to the fish. It does have a wider depth range than most people give it credit for. It has the 'walking the dog' type of action of a Zara Spook that's actually done under the water at a level where the fish are. You can also hover the bait – stop it and almost suspend it, which is attractive to larger fish."

Unaltered, most jerkbaits can be powered down to 5 to 7 feet, where they can be twitched and maneuvered for a few seconds before quickly returning to the surface. What the pros discovered was that by weighting a jerkbait, it could be driven down as deep as 15 feet and, when paused, practically suspend while being manipulated to walk in a side-to-side manner for a surprising period of time.

That unique suspending action proved to be irresistible to bass that had never seen such a movement at such a depth. And the grapevine on the professional tournament circuits began to buzz with excitement.

The pros began experimenting with various ways to add enough weight to the hard-plastic lures to make them suspend – a delicate balancing act in itself. Most efforts involved inserting lead into the body of the jerkbait or placing lead wrap around the hook holders.

Rick Clunn

Rick Clunn is the only four-time winner of the coveted BASS Masters Classic – an event he has qualified for a record 24 consecutive times. He has won 20 tournaments on various circuits, including three that carried a $100,000 check. A member of bass-fishing's millionaire's club, Clunn lives in Montgomery, Texas.

A slowly rising jerk-bait is deadly on early season bass.

Although some of the pros still rely on their own modified baits, most major minnowbait manufacturers are now marketing some type of weighted jerkbait.

When & Where to Fish Weighted Jerkbaits

The weighted jerkbait has a reputation as a coldwater lure. It's generally considered to be most effective at water temperatures in the 40 to 60°F range.

Clayton Douglass, a veteran tournament competitor from Oklahoma, believes weight-ed jerkbaits are most effective in the spring. In fact, they may be the deadliest pre-spawn lures of all.

"In a pre-spawn situation, the fish are suspended a lot – especially in clear water," Douglass explains. "They may be in water that is 30 feet deep, but they'll suspend down 15 feet or so. This bait will go down to 15 feet and then will slowly float up. The water is so cold that these fish don't want to chase anything. But when something stops right in front of them and floats up real slow, they can't resist it."

Although Rick Clunn agrees that weight-ed jerkbaits are at their best in the pre-through post-spawn situations, he emphasizes that it is a mistake to limit their usage to the spring of the year.

"I've used weighted jerkbaits out in Lake Mead in the hot summer on windy bluffs," he adds. "And it's a good fall bait. At the MegaBucks tournament in October (on South Carolina's Lake Murray), a lot of guys were catching their fish by jerking a jerkbait. Later in the fall at Lake Texoma (on the Texas/Oklahoma border), one of the anglers who finished high caught all of his fish by fishing behind me with a jerkbait."

Weighted jerkbaits work best in waters with at least moderate clarity. Their success depends mainly on visual attraction, so they are usually not effective where the visibility is less than 2 feet.

Selecting Weighted Jerkbaits

One of the first pros to experiment with modifying jerkbaits was Clayton Douglass. He developed a thriving black-market business selling weighted Smithwick Rattlin' Rogues for a whopping $45 each. Douglass' creations were used by some of the top finishers in the now-famous Kentucky Lake tournament.

Although Douglass' handiwork is still in demand, weighted jerkbaits are now available from a variety of

Popular Weighted Jerkbaits

manufacturers, including Smithwick, Rapala, Rebel, Bomber, Storm and others. They come in a variety of sizes and have different types of lips, which determine how deep they will dive.

Shallow-running models have a short lip that is angled sharply downward; they run at depths of less than 4 feet. Deep runners have a long lip that is angled only slightly; they reach depths of 8 to 15 feet. Medium runners have intermediate lips and run at depths of 4 to 8 feet.

Buoyancy is another important consideration. "There are times when you want the bait to rise and other times when you want it to sink and just sit there," says Clunn. "Some weighted jerkbait makers may label their lures as neutrally buoyant, but that's bull. Those baits can only be neutrally buoyant at one certain water temperature. But water temperatures change, which means the density of the water changes.

"Today's buoyancy may not be the same as tomorrow's. So that means you have to readjust [your bait] to it. The hotter the water, the less dense it is, so you don't need as much weight. The colder the water, the more dense it is and the more weight you need in the bait. If the lead-weighted bait is truly neutrally buoyant in 60-degree water, once you get into the summer months, that

Rapala
Husky Jerk

Smithwick
Rattlin' Rogue

R.I.P. 'n Ric

Storm
Thunder Stick

bait is going to be a sinker. And if it's sinking, you can't take the weight off.

"There are a lot of ways to weight a jerkbait, but none of them are easy or convenient. And once you weight a jerkbait by inserting lead or using lead wrap, it is real hard – if not impossible – to make any adjustment on the water."

Frustration with modifying hard-plastic jerkbaits prompted Clunn to design the R.I.P. 'n Ric, which has a hollow cavity in the middle of the lure that serves as a ballast chamber. To adjust the buoyancy, you simply add or drain water. The bait comes with a syringe that fits into a small valve (similar to that of a basketball) in the belly of the lure.

Fishing a Weighted Jerkbait

"Regardless of the season," says Clunn, "the most important thing about fishing a weighted jerkbait is paying attention to how the first few fish react to the bait. Are they hitting it on the dead still or are they reacting to it when it starts to float up? The real

key with these baits is being aware of how the fish want it worked."

The only sure way to determine what the fish want on a given day is to experiment. Start with the basic stop-and-go presentation. After making a long cast, point your rod tip at the water and give the bait a series of alternating sharp twitches and pauses. The bait will dart erratically, then stop and hang motionless. Be ready for a strike on the pause.

Vary the length and frequency of twitches and the duration of pauses until you find what the fish want. Some pros hesitate as long as 30 seconds between twitches, but there are times when the fish prefer practically no hesitation.

Be sure to choose a lure that will dive to the depths where you expect the fish to be holding. The lure's diving ability is not as much of a consideration in very clear water, because the bass can see the lure from a distance and swim up to grab it.

Another consideration is buoyancy. Most pros prefer a lure that rests motionless when

To achieve the proper action, angle your rod tip at the water, as shown, and retrieve with a series of downward jerks.

you stop reeling. That's what usually appeals to finicky bass. But if you're fishing over heavy weeds or brush, you may want a lure that floats up slowly. And if you're trying to reach deep cover, you probably want a bait that sinks a little.

There are times when bass will slam a weighted jerkbait but, more often, all you feel is a subtle tick or just a little extra resistance. Whenever you feel anything out of the ordinary, crank up the slack and set the hook with a firm, sideways sweep of the rod.

Weighted jerkbaits are now part of the arsenal of every pro bass angler. So toss out some of those rusty baits and make a place for them in your tackle box.

How to Modify Jerkbaits

Although some excellent weighted jerkbaits are now available, you should know how to modify them so they suspend properly at different water temperatures.

Clayton Douglass modifies his jerkbaits by drilling holes in the body and inserting just enough lead to give it the correct level balance. When weighted properly, Douglass' baits rise very slowly, taking about 70 seconds to float to the surface from a depth of 12 feet.

But drilling holes in a bait and inserting lead is a time-consuming process. Douglass spends about three hours on each bait. Here are some simpler ways to weight jerkbaits:

How to Weight a Jerkbait

Place stick-on lead disks, called SuspenDots, on the lure's belly, distributing them so as not to upset the head-to-tail balance. If you can't find these dots, you can use small pieces of golfer's tape.

The R.I.P. 'n Ric, designed by Rick Clunn, has an internal water chamber; water can be added or removed with a syringe.

After removing the rubber inserts from small Rubber-cor sinkers, pinch the remaining split lead weights onto the front and middle hooks. Trim the lead as needed for neutral buoyancy.

Wrap the upper shank of the treble hooks with fine-diameter solder. Put equal amounts of lead on each hook so you don't upset the lure's balance. Tank-test the lure until it is neutrally buoyant.

Crankin' Stripers

by Don Wirth

Thin fog shrouded the lake as I approached the cove, moving silently under trolling motor power. Up ahead I could hear the familiar percussive slaps of big stripers pulverizing shad on the surface. I knew if I could get within casting distance quickly, a hookup with a good fish would be guaranteed.

I picked up a rod rigged with a big Cordell Redfin and made a long cast into the fog. The lure splatted loudly on impact and I began a slow, steady retrieve back to the boat, keeping the Redfin wobbling on top in an enticing manner. It traveled perhaps 10 feet when a rolling wave appeared to the left as a big striper made its move for the lure. I braced myself for the strike, but none came. Instead, the fish boiled beneath the lure once, twice, refusing to take it.

I cast again, retrieving the Redfin on the surface for the second time. Through the thinning fog, I could make out silvery flashes beneath the lure as an entire school of stripers followed it, still refusing to strike. In frustration, I began reeling in quickly to change to a big propbait, something a bit noisier and more aggravating. That's when I learned something about stripers.

When I began speed-reeling the lure, it dove beneath the surface and gyrated crazily as it moved toward me. Within three feet it was clobbered not by one, but two big stripers! I immediately knew what I had, for upon impact, both fish sloshed on top, their huge tails slapping the surface. Ten minutes later I had them both in the boat, and my arms felt like jelly from the battle. One fish weighed 27 pounds, the other 33. "Well, you finally did it – you always said you wanted to catch a 60-pounder some day!" my fishing partner laughed.

We hung around that cove until mid-morning, when the sun burned off the fog and the stripers moved deep. Only this time, instead of trying to tempt stripers with a surface presentation, we dug through our tackle boxes for big crankbaits. While crankin', I caught two more fish that morning in the 30-pound class; my friend tagged a 37-pounder and had his line broken by an even bigger fish.

On that foggy morning, the fish were telling me something in their refusal to blast my Redfin on the surface. They were surely attracted to the lure, as was evidenced by their rolling wakes, angry swirls and flushing boils all around it. They came within an inch of actually striking it, but something held them back.

Only when I cranked the bait under the surface did I connect with a fish. The stripers clearly didn't want a topwater presentation that morning, they wanted a crankbait.

Don Wirth

Besides being a well-known outdoor writer and boating industry consultant, Don Wirth is an accomplished striped bass fisherman and guide. He is considered one of the country's leading authorities on this exciting gamefish.

Wirth lives in Nashville, Tennessee.

Day in and day out, live-bait fishing is easily the most dependable way to catch striped bass. But if you're like me and get a special charge out of having one of these bruisers blast an artificial lure, you need to spend more time crankin'.

Choosing Crankbaits for Stripers

Your crankbait selection depends on the striper potential of the waters you're fishing. In reservoirs and rivers where small stripers (10 pounds or less) are the rule, stick with bass-sized crankbaits. These baits work great for hybrids as well. Where there's a good possibility of monster stripers – fish in excess of 30 pounds – forget bass-sized cranks, relying instead on the biggest striper and muskie models. And make sure they're equipped with heavy-duty hooks and hardware.

You need a much more limited selection of crankbait colors when gunning for stripers than when fishing for bass. Silvery or bone-colored lures work well under most conditions; these imitate schooling baitfish, including threadfin

and gizzard shad. I've found highly reflective finishes work best on bright days in clear water, where their flash is maximized. But in low-light conditions in clear water, you'll get more strikes if you switch to flat white, pearl or bone. Another good clear-water color is rainbow trout. Red, perch and chartreuse will catch fish in murky water, and black works at night and under foggy or rainy conditions.

Here's a rundown on the types of crankbaits used by striper fishermen:

Floating/diving minnows – These all share the long, slender profile of soft-rayed baitfish species including shad and herring, the preferred forage fish of landlocked stripers. Most are available in a variety of sizes and depth ranges, from shallow-running to deep-diving.

Suspending minnows or "jerkbaits" – These are marketed mainly to bass anglers, but will catch stripers as well, especially in clear reservoirs. Their ability to suspend allows the angler to fish them very slowly, an advantage in cold water.

Giant bass plugs – These huge plugs, some more than a foot long, are currently in vogue among lunker largemouth hunters, particularly in California and Texas. Surprise – they were originally invented for striper

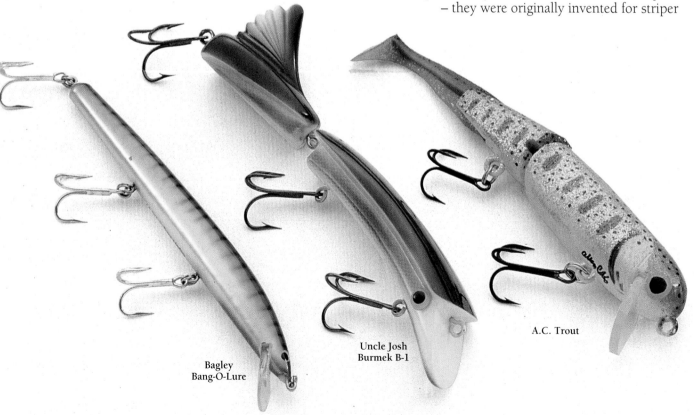

Bagley
Bang-O-Lure

Uncle Josh
Burmek B-1

A.C. Trout

Rapala
Husky Jerk

Mann
Dancer

Rapala
Shad Rap

Bill Lewis
Super-Trap

fishing. They're shallow-divers with a wildly errat-ic action. Many are jointed and painted to resemble a rainbow trout, a favorite striper forage in some reservoirs and tailraces. Drawback: These plugs are expensive, routinely costing $20 or more, and stripers are notorious line-busters.

Potbellied bass crankbaits – The mainstay of bass anglers, these baits are capable of tagging big stripers as well. Their potbellied design suggests a live bluegill, another forage species popular with landlocked stripers. Available in depth ranges from shallow to super-deep, they work surprisingly well for stripers when trolled.

Lipless rattling crankbaits – These noisy shallow-divers are among the most versatile crankbaits you can use for stripers, and will produce jarring strikes with a rapid retrieve. The Bill Lewis Super-Trap, an oversized model with super-strong hooks and hardware, is one of my favorites.

Metal crankbaits – This relatively new crankbait category offers the serious striper angler some interesting possibilities. Metal cranks have maximum flash, making them highly visible in clear water. They're also highly wind-resistant and can be cast a country mile.

Muskie crankbaits & trolling plugs – Stripers and muskies are two of our largest inland gamefish, yet I've been amazed at how rarely big, heavy-duty muskie lures have been used for striper fishing. These plugs have the size and action needed to draw strikes from massive stripers and, even better, they've got extra-heavy hooks and hardware to withstand their powerhouse runs.

Crankin' Stripers: A Seasonal Approach

Stripers are nomads; their lengthy seasonal movements make it difficult for the average angler to keep up with them. Here are some tips that will help you find stripers throughout the year:

Early Spring – Monitor water temperatures carefully, looking for the warmest water you can find that isn't muddy. Stripers have a disdain for muddy water and will stay ahead of it as it washes into the reservoir via the tributaries after spring floods. Although the fish cannot spawn successfully in most reservoirs, they make an attempt to

Recommended Tackle

Tackle selection depends upon lure size and striper-size potential. A 6½- to 7-foot, medium- to medium-heavy-power graphite rod is a good all-around choice. The long rod gives you extra casting distance and fish-handling ability. Pair this rod with a sturdy baitcasting reel spooled with 20- to 40-pound-test mono. Stripers aren't particularly line-shy, even in gin-clear water, and the heavier mono will minimize break offs of expensive crankbaits.

For smaller stripers, drop down to 14- to 20-pound mono; for big stripers in snaggy rivers, use 40- to 50-pound.

Superlines are not recommended for striper crankin'. The lack of stretch will cause monster stripers to break your rod, pull the hooks out of your lure or rip the hooks out of themselves.

Stripers hit and then fight hard, so make sure your baits are equipped with heavy-duty hooks and hardware.

spawn. They start moving toward their spawning grounds, usually in the tailwaters of the upstream dam, when the lake warms into the lower 50s. Spawning activity takes place around 65°F.

As they move, stripers stop and feed along key main-lake structures, especially long, slow-tapering points that eventually connect with the deep river channel. A good bet is to check these points beginning in the middle of the reservoir, working progressive-ly uplake until you locate schools of stripers. Any of the crankbaits mentioned may produce strikes here, but until you've pinpoint-ed fish, either troll crankbaits on flatlines, targeting the 5- to 15-foot zone, or position your boat in the middle of the point and fan-cast crankbaits. Some fish may stay on long points and attempt to spawn there rather than move into the headwaters.

Spring – As the water temperature approaches 60°F, target shallow points in the

Where to Find Stripers

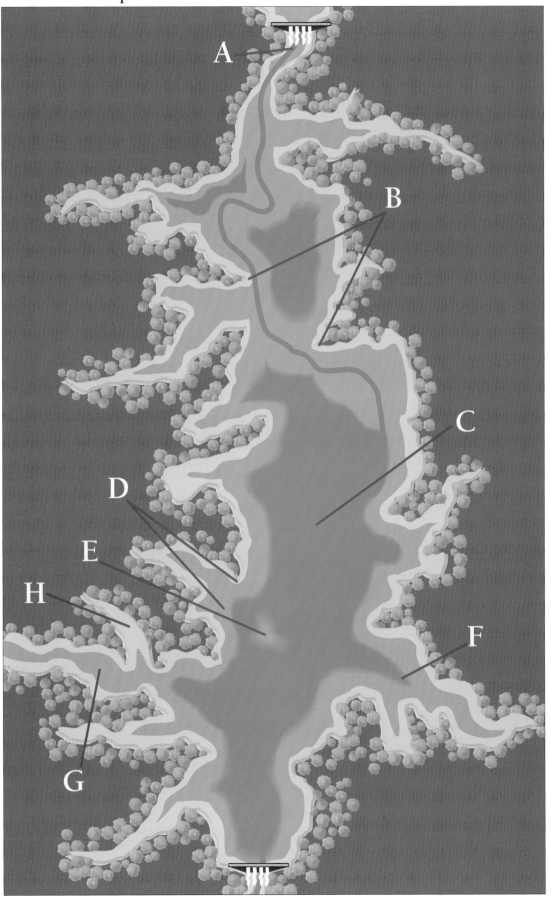

Stripers spawn in (A) the tailwaters of the upstream dam. Then, they move downstream, stopping at (B) main-lake points that connect with the main inner channel. In summer, you'll find stripers suspended over (C) the deepest part of the lake. In fall, you'll find stripers on (D) long main-lake points, (E) on humps, and (F) in deep creek arms. In winter, the fish seek out flats in (G) shallow creek arms and in (H) secondary creek arms.

When you find stripers busting into schools of shad on the surface, cast well past them with a shallow-running minnowbait and reel it through the area where the fish are breaking.

Try working a floating minnowbait, such as a Cordell Redfin, just beneath the surface so it makes a noticeable wake that imitates a struggling shad. Experiment with your retrieve speed and rod angle to achieve the desired effect.

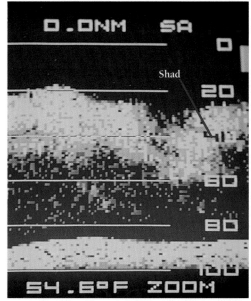

Locate stripers in deeper water by looking for schools of shad on your graph. When you find a mass of shad, tie on a crankbait that will run just above them. Stripers are more likely to come up for a bait than go down for it.

upper end of the reservoir with shallow-divers, such as the Redfin and Long A. Clear, flowing water attracts spawning fish, so don't be afraid to venture into the extreme shallows upriver. If these areas are muddy, move back downlake until you find clear water, then cast crankbaits to humps and points.

Summer – This is trolling time in reservoirs. Stripers are likely to be deep; locate the thermocline on your graph and notice the depth of suspending baitfish schools and stripers. Then troll just above this depth – stripers will seldom go deeper to take a lure.

Where legal, trolling multiple lines at different depths is the best plan. For example, run one lure around 12 feet, a second at 22 feet and a third at 30 feet. Troll across primary main-lake structures, especially humps and points (both shallow and deep), around islands and along bluff banks. All of these spots attract baitfish. Concentrate on the midsection of the lake down to the dam. Stripers are likely to be sluggish in warm water, so don't troll too fast.

Fall – This is a time of transition for stripers. In deep, clear reservoirs, the water remains warm for long periods in early fall, usually necessitating trolling presentations. Troll a bit faster and move your lures progressively shallower as the water cools. When it drops to the mid-60s, fish move much shallower and will be catchable early and late in the day on long main-lake points and humps, and in the deeper creek arms. Feeding activity is likely to be intense now, so a fast-moving crankbait presentation should draw savage strikes.

Winter – When the water temperature drops into the mid-50s, stripers move shallow and gorge themselves on baitfish. Key on flats and in shallow creek arms, usually in the lower third of the reservoir, and cast the shad-imitating crankbait of your choice. Lipless models work especially well now; these can be bumped off shallow stumps and rocks without hanging up. As the temperature gradually dips into the 40s, use a progressively slower retrieve and a more realistic lure, like a Redfin or Long A. Stripers will slam crankbaits in shallow water until the water temperature drops to around 40 degrees. At the tail-end of the season, downsize to bass-sized crankbaits reeled very slowly.

Next time out, take my advice and try crankin' for stripers. Trust me, when a big fish appears out of nowhere and blasts your crankbait so hard the rod buckles and your arms ache, the fish won't be the only thing that's hooked!

Crankin' Stripers in Rivers
by Don Wirth

My biggest stripers come from rivers. Here are some tricks I've learned that can help you crank up a monster from moving water.

• Knock on wood – Bass anglers know crankbaits catch more fish when they're bumped off woody cover, and this approach works on stripers as well. River stripers use submerged trees as current breaks and predatorial ambush points. Either a lipless crankbait or one with a long diving lip will bump off logs easily and can produce a jolting strike from a big-river striper.

• Fish 'em fast – In gin-clear rivers, I've found the longer a striper has to eyeball your lure, the more likely it is to reject it. A fast retrieve usually draws far more strikes than a slow one, even in cold water.

• Jerk 'em – Most crankbaits have a repetitive, built-in action. This is fine in murky rivers, but you'll find it's a drawback in clear tailraces. Stripers may reject the lure when it doesn't appear to attempt escape as they approach it. In clear water, always intersperse the retrieve with sharp jerks of the rod tip to give the lure a more realistic, erratic action. If you spot a striper bird-dogging the lure, rip the bait with a sharp sweep of the rod tip; this will make it dart wildly like a fleeing baitfish and often provokes an instant strike.

• Tight-line 'em – Sometimes the current is too swift to facilitate adequate casting coverage. Try anchoring in heavy current, then casting a crankbait upstream and tight-lining it as it sweeps downriver. If you don't get a strike, lift the anchor, drift downstream 20 to 40 yards and repeat.

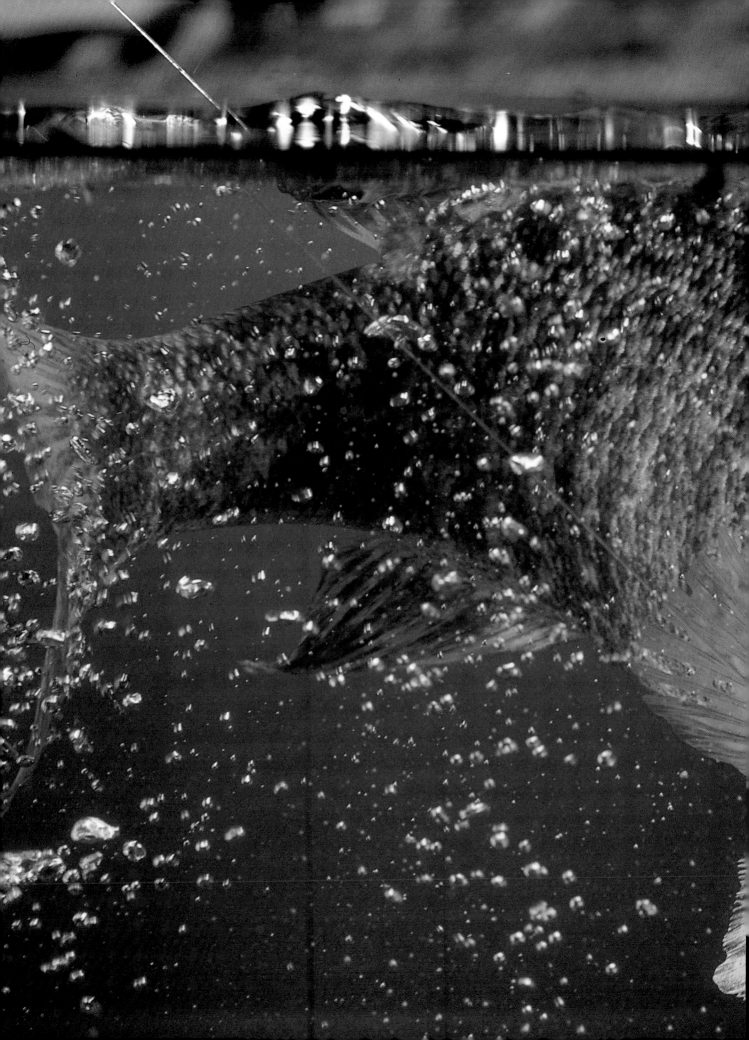

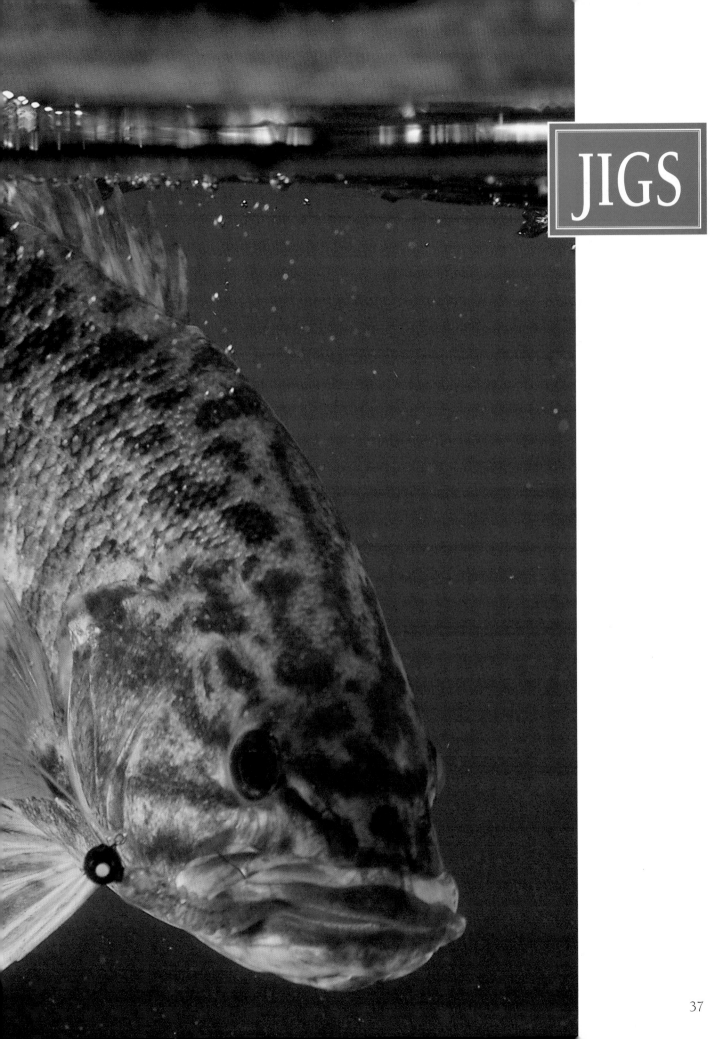

JIGS

Hair Jigs & Grubs
The Forgotten Baits

By Don Wirth

There are any number of ways to fool trophy bass. In California, the current craze is throwing giant crankbaits, some of which cost as much as dinner for two at a fancy restaurant, for those potbellied 20-pounders (pp. 16-21).

At the opposite end of the scale in terms of both size and price are hair jigs and grubs. These "lowly" artificials seldom get much press in outdoor magazines, yet they probably account for as many monster bass as those huge California plugs.

Hair jigs are among the earliest styles of artificial lures. They are simple, basic baits that will catch just about anything that swims, including all species of bass.

At one time, "bucktails" (another name for hair jigs) were extremely popular among bass fishermen. These early hair jigs were basic leadhead lures to which deer hair was tied as a hook dressing. But in the late sixties, tournament fishing grew popular, and pro anglers began using rubber-legged jigs to catch huge strings of largemouths. Two radical presentations, flipping and pitching, were invented especially for these weedless lures, and soon many weekend bassers had forgotten hair jigs in favor of rubber-legged jigs. Today, hair jigs and grubs are most often used by smallmouth anglers, although they will definitely catch big largemouths as well.

Grubs are more recent fishing innovations than hair jigs. Soft-plastic lures didn't take off until the "Bass Boom" of the late sixties. Around 1970, the Mister Twister screw-tail grub was introduced; it is still considered the gold standard of grub designs by most bass anglers.

Goodlettsville, Tennessee, bass guide Jack Christian is a master with both hair jigs and grubs. These deadly little baits are capable of amazing bass-catching feats when worked properly in the right spots. Here, Christian reveals the secrets of fishing these lures to NAFC members.

When & Where to Fish Hair Jigs & Grubs

Both hair jigs and grubs can be fished in virtually the same places for big bass. Here are some spots to try:

Spawning flats – In early spring, smallmouth bass move out of deep water onto slow-tapering gravel or clay flats to spawn. You'll typically find them in 5 to 12 feet of water, depending on clarity. Largemouth will spawn on flats, too, but they prefer sand- or mud-bottomed flats with isolated patches of weeds. Largemouth typically spawn a little later in the spring and in much shallower water (1 to 3 feet).

Sloping banks – Look for banks that descend into deep water at a 45-degree angle and are composed of rock. Fish them in fall and winter.

Jack Christian

Jack Christian is considered one of the South's top multi-species guides. He honed his angling skills on Percy Priest and Old Hickory reservoirs near Nashville, Tennessee, where he now guides for largemouth, stripers and hybrids. His specialty, however, is light-tackle fishing for smallmouth.

Christian makes his home in Goodlettsville, Tennessee.

Hair jigs are hard to beat for coldwater bass.

Deep ledges – These are common in most reservoirs and are usually associated with a creek or river channel. Try them in hot weather, especially at night.

Rockpiles, humps and other "high spots" – These are usually located offshore and pull in bass from a wide area. They are good pre-spawn staging areas in early spring, and will usually hold fish in hot weather as well.

Hair jigs and grubs work best in clear water that's relatively free of obstructions.

They're not recommended in some typical bass-holding spots, such as stumpy backwaters or weedy coves. In heavy cover like this, you're far better off fishing a spinnerbait or a flipping jig with a brushguard.

Hair jigs are among the very best lures you can use in cold, clear water. "I've caught big bass on them in water as cold as 37 degrees, says Christian, "and in lakes so clear you could read the date on a dime at 15 feet. By contrast, rubber-legged flipping jigs will usually work better in murky water, when the water is warm, and when bass are holding in thick weed or wood cover.

"Many anglers use a grub interchangeably with a hair jig. However my personal preference is to fish a hair jig in the coldest water, then switch over to a grub when the water temperature hits around 58 degrees in the spring. I've found a grub to be slightly more effective in warmer water – during the daylight hours, that is.

"Most night bass anglers in my area fish a hair jig, but I've found a grub to work just as well. Try both to see which works best on your home lakes."

Spear-tail Grub   Plain Hair Jig   Shad-tail Grub   Curly-tail Grub

Fly 'n' Rind   Spider Jig   Hair Jig with Pork Chunk

Selecting the Right Jig

HAIR JIGS – This category includes any jig tied with a tail of natural or synthetic hair. Deer hair (bucktail) is the most popular tail material, for good reason. The fibers are hollow, giving the tail a lifelike "breathing" action.

Hair jigs are often, but not always, fished with a trailer, most commonly a small pork frog, strip or eel. "In Tennessee, where I fish," says Christian, "the combination of a hair jig and pork is known locally as a 'fly 'n' rind.' This is the way I fish my hair jigs most of the time—with a pork trailer.

You can also rig a hair jig with a soft-plastic trailer, such as a slender split-tail eel, crayfish imitation or curly-tail grub. And many anglers tip their hair jigs with live bait, anything from a small minnow to a live leech to a wriggly spring lizard (salamander).

"A trailer can help you fine-tune your presentation," says Christian. "Some anglers like to use a trailer that's the same color as their jig—example: black jig, black trailer. I like to vary the two colors slightly to create a little contrast – black jig, brown trailer or vice-versa. In murky water, you can put a hot-colored trailer, like chartreuse or orange, on a dark-colored jig for maximum visibility.

"Sometimes it's better to fish a hair jig all by itself. When the bite is really slow on the coldest winter days, a plain jig can outfish

one with a trailer 2 to 1. I also like a plain hair jig in current, because it creates less drag on the line and sinks into the strike zone more quickly than one with a trailer."

GRUBS – There are dozens of styles of soft-plastic grubs that can be rigged on a jig-head. All of them will catch bass, but the following four styles are most effective:

Curly-tail – This is, by far, the most popular style. Also called a screw-tail or twister-tail, it has a puffy body and a curly, flexible tail that creates a rippling effect when the lure is retrieved.

Spear tail – Although most commonly used in salt water, this grub style will also catch bass, especially schooling fish.

Shad tail – This style has a blunt, water-grabbing tail that causes the grub to writhe in a lifelike manner when retrieved. It's most effective in current because it sinks quickly and resembles a fast-moving baitfish.

Spider jig – This style combines a curly-tail grub with a collar studded with soft plastic legs. When a bass inhales the spider

These small baits account for surprising numbers of big bass.

needed, switch to a ⅛-ounce. In extremely deep water, try a ½-ounce.

Grubs are available in literally hundreds of color combinations, but you only need a few to catch bass consistently. In early spring, when the water is cold and somewhat murky from seasonal rains, a dark-colored grub such as brown or pumpkin pepper works well. In clear water on a sunny day, use a light-colored grub such as smoke or clear sparkle. In clear water on a cloudy day, or any time the water is dingy, try chartreuse.

How to Fish Hair Jigs & Grubs

Here are a few basic retrieves you need to know when fishing a hair jig or grub. Each retrieve works well with either lure.

Swimming Retrieve – Use this retrieve in spring, when bass have moved out of their deep winter haunts and are either spawning or staging up to spawn. It works best in fairly shallow water (from 2 to around 12 feet).

First, make a long cast past the target and let the jig or grub sink to the bottom. Then, raise the rod tip to the 10 o'clock position and begin reeling slowly and steadily so the lure "swims" back to the boat.

Occasionally stop and let the lure fall back to the bottom, then begin reeling again. If you feel the lure drag bottom, speed up the retrieve a bit.

Spring bass are often sluggish. A strike may feel like you've hooked a leaf or weed. If you feel any resistance, set the hook!

Pop-n-Drop – This retrieve is dynamite in the winter, when bass are holding on steep rocky banks.

With your boat in deep water, cast to the bank. Let the lure hit bottom while holding your rod steady at 10 to 11 o'clock.

Lower the rod tip a little while reeling in slack line, give the rod tip a slight pop, and then return it to 10 or 11 o'clock while the lure sinks to the next level.

Continue this procedure to walk the jig down the slope. If you see the line twitch or feel a tap, set the hook.

jig, the legs and collar feel extremely lifelike and the fish often will not let go.

In most situations, a 4- or 5-inch grub will catch plenty of bass of all sizes. A grub in this size range mimics a broad array of forage. Use smaller grubs in cold water or any time the bite is very slow; larger grubs, in murky water or when really big bass are likely.

As a rule, start with a ¼-ounce leadhead. In cold water where a slower sink rate is

The Ledge Crawl – This retrieve works well when bass are located along a ledge or channel drop-off. Deep ledges (12 to 30 feet) are best for smallmouth; shallow ledges (8 to 15 feet), for largemouth.

With your boat positioned on the deep side of a ledge, cast the jig or grub to the shallowest part of the structure. Let the lure hit bottom with the rod tip at 10 o'clock. Lower the rod tip so it is just a few inches above the surface, s-l-o-w-l-y turn the reel handle a few times, then stop. Continue reeling and stopping until the lure falls off the ledge. Bass often suspend at this drop-off.

Once the lure has dropped off the edge, swim it slowly and steadily a few feet. This will often attract any fish that are suspended in the channel. Set the hook when you feel any resistance.

Four Tips for Fishing Hair Jigs & Grubs

Add a rattle to your jig when fishing discolored water. This type of rattle slips over the collar of your jig head.

Bend the point of your jig hook to the side to improve your hooking percentage. This way, the point is more likely to catch in the fish's jaw.

Use a jig with a thin-wire hook when fishing in woody cover. Then, should you get snagged, a straight pull will bend the hook enough to free the bait.

Add a larger soft-plastic tail to slow your jig's sink rate. When bass are finicky, they're more likely to take a slower-sinking bait.

Recommended Tackle

For fishing hair jigs and grubs, Christian prefers a 6-foot to 6-foot, 4-inch, medium-heavy-power, fast-action graphite spinning rod.

A lighter rod prevents you from detecting light biters and makes it hard to get a solid hook set. A heavier rod is too much stick for the light line you'll be using most of the time.

Spool a regular-sized spinning reel (not an ultralight) with 6- or 8-pound-test, abrasion-resistant mono. Fluorescent mono is recommended because it allows you to see the small-diameter line more easily and detect light bites. At night, Christian uses fluorescent line in combination with a black light, which causes even the lightest fluorescent lines to look like thick neon tubing and makes it easy to see even the slightest twitch when a bass takes the lure.

Secrets of the Bass Pros

43

Roll'r Jigging

The $200,000 Technique

by Dick Sternberg

Used to be, Jim Moynagh was a shallow-water fisherman. "The best kind of tournament" he would say, "is one where you don't have to turn on your depth finder."

Moynagh, then an emerging star in Midwest bass-fishing circles, was winning his share of regional tournaments, but he soon began to realize that his shallow-water approach had its limitations. "In conversations with walleye experts, I kept hearing of huge catches of big bass taken on deep rock piles – places I rarely fished," he reminisced.

Then, Moynagh had a chance to fish with western pros, Ted Miller and Randy Best, who introduced him to the football jig. "I was really impressed with the rocking motion of the jig, the way it hugged bottom and how much the movement resembled that of a crayfish," Moynagh said.

"I took some of the jigs home and started playing around with them. I was surprised at how well they worked for catching big bass off deep rock piles in my home lakes. But there were some things I didn't like about the football jigs that were on the market. The hooks were way too light; they were opening up and I was losing too many fish. The problem is, when a bass takes this type of bait, it almost always heads straight to the surface and tries to throw it. When I tried to put enough pressure on the fish to hold it down, the hook would bend. Another problem was that the exposed hook eye tended to catch weeds."

Moynagh contacted a local lure manufacturer and, together, they came up with an improved design "We replaced the fine-wire hook with a heavy Owner's Flippin' Hook, we molded a groove into the head to recess the hook eye, and we modified the head to look like a crayfish tail. We also gave it a knobby texture which, in some situations, makes it grip the bottom better and improves the kicking action."

Using prototypes of this new jig, Moynagh shocked the bass-fishing world by outdistancing a field including many of the nation's top pros in the Don Shelby Invitational, held on Minnesota's Lake Minnetonka. Moynagh's three-day limit (15 bass) weighed 68.24 pounds for an astounding 4.55-pound average. The catch earned him $50,000 and launched his pro-bass fishing career.

Ecstatic about the performance of the new jig, Moynagh gave the okay to Walker Fishing Systems of Navarre, Minnesota, to market the "Roll'r Rock Jig." Most anglers refer to the bait simply as the "Roll'r Jig."

To firmly cement the Roll'r Jig's place in bass-fishing history, Moynagh used it to anchor a catch of decent-size crankbait-caught bass and win the Forrest L. Wood Open on Lake Minnetonka the next year. By 9 a.m. on the final day, Moynagh had a pair of crankbait bass in his livewell. "I knew I couldn't win with 3 more bass that size. I figured I had almost 6 hours to get three bites on the Roll'r Jig, so I made the switch.

Jim Moynagh

Jim Moynagh has used his training in fisheries biology and the knowledge gained from years of making fishing books to fuel his spectacular rise in the pro-bass rankings. A serious student of bass behavior, Moynagh is known for his clutch performances in big-money tournaments.

Moynagh resides in Hopkins, Minnesota.

I caught a 4-plus pounder on the first spot I tried it."

But then Moynagh had a long dry spell, so he went back to crankin, and landed one more 2-plus pounder. With only 40 minutes to go, he decided to go for broke and give the Roll'r Jig another try. With the clock ticking down to 20 minutes, a 3-pound, 9-ouncer inhaled the jig and gave Moynagh the weight he needed to claim the $200,000 first prize – the largest in the history of tournament bass fishing.

When & Where to Roll'r Jig

"The Roll'r Jig is a great big-fish bait," Moynagh claims. "The large head and the skirted twin-tail dressing give it a big, crawdad-like profile. Plus, the deeper, clean-bottomed lips where I fish it tend to hold bigger bass.

"But you can't use the bait everywhere. You've got to have a clean bottom – either sand, gravel or rock. If the lake is all silted in or if the bottom is covered with spriggly weeds like sand grass, Roll'r jigging is a waste of time."

Although Moynagh does most of his Roll'r jigging in fairly deep water, depth is not as important as weed growth "In dirty water, the weedline might be only five foot," he says, "so I'll be fishing from five foot on out."

When Roll'r jigging, Moynagh looks for points, especially those with an extended lip of sand, gravel or rock. He also finds fish on inside turns, but saddles are his favorite type of structure. "A saddle is the king of all structure," Moynagh contends, "especially if it has a big weed flat on either end." It was on a spot like this that Moynagh won the 1995 Don Shelby Invitational.

Time of year is not much of a factor, although Moynagh does not Roll'r jig during the spawning period, when bass are in shallow, weedy or brushy cover. He prefers overcast days and has noticed that a series of cloudy days pushes bass out of dense weeds and onto a clean bottom, where they can easily be Roll'r jigged. Early morning

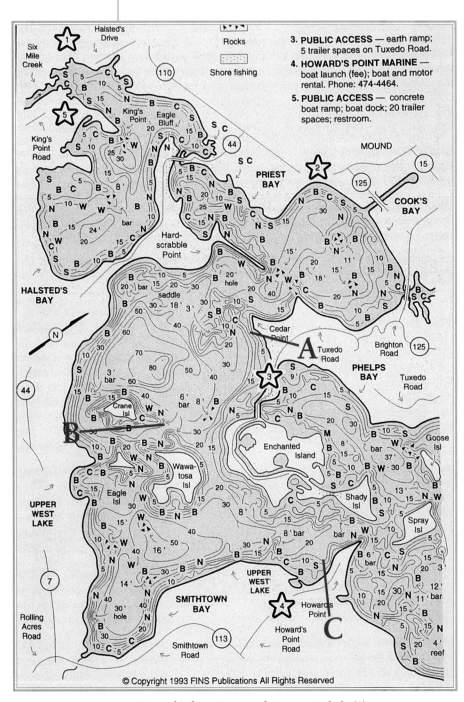

Moynagh's favorite types of structure include (A) saddles, (B) sand-gravel points with an extended lip, and (C) inside turns in the weedline.

Jigging / Roll'r Jigging: The $200,000 Technique

The tip-up action of a Roll'r Jig resembles a cray in a defensive position.

is a key time, but the technique will work all day.

"I've had my best success when the fish were glued to the bottom and feeding down," Moynagh notes. "Sometimes they seem to be riding a little higher and looking up for their food. Then, you're better off with a crankbait or a slow-rolled spinner-bait."

"The bait makes a lot of commotion as it clunks along the bottom, so it really works well in murky water. I think the bass hear it, so they swim over to check it out. But I catch plenty of fish on it in clear water, too.

Gearing Up

A "football-head" jig is a must for this technique, because its shape gives you the unique crayfish-like, tip-up action. There are several football-head jigs on the market that can be used for Roll'r jigging, but Moynagh

Moynagh prefers a 7½-foot, heavy power, fast-action flippin stick with "just a little tip to it." A long rod is necessary to take up the stretch of mono on long casts. It also helps take up the slack created when a bass picks up the jig and swims toward you.

A high-speed reel also helps take up slack quickly and is important for solid hook sets and quickly reeling in to get rid of weeds.

Spool up with 20-pound limp monofilament; lighter line has too much stretch for a solid hook set, especially at the end of a long cast. Superlines will also work for Roll'r jigging, but you lose the "rubber band" effect that mono gives you (p. 49).

prefers the Roll'r Rock Jig he helped develop, because of the subtle differences mentioned earlier.

Roll'r Jigs come in ½- and ¾-ounce sizes; other types of football jigs are available in sizes as light as ¼ ounce. Moynagh sticks with the ¾-ounce size, because it's easy to cast long distances and it hugs the bottom.

Roll'r Jigs come dressed with a skirted twin-tail or a silicone jig skirt. You can also buy plain Roll'r Jig heads and rig them with your own dressing, such as a live-rubber jig skirt or plastic craw. The latter is a good option in dirty water, because of its larger profile.

"The best colors are earth tones," Moynagh contends. "I like black, blue and black, green, pumpkin, watermelon and various shades of brown. In clear water, a translucent trailer works best; in murky water, I go with a solid color, usually black or maybe black and chartreuse.

Besides the right bait and tackle, you also need a good depth finder that enables you to distinguish a soft bottom from a hard one. "It doesn't matter whether it's a graph or a flasher, as long as you know how to read it," Moynagh says. "I like a flasher because I

don't have to spend as much time adjusting it to get a good reading."

The Roll'r Jigging Technique

A Roll'r Jig is one of the best-ever crayfish imitations. It's not so much that it looks like a crayfish but, fished properly, it moves a like a crayfish.

"The technique is really pretty simple, although lots of fishermen have a hard time figuring it out," Moynagh says. "They fish the bait for maybe a half hour, then put it away without ever really giving it a chance.

"When I first tried a football jig, what impressed me most was how well it worked for locating rocks. And finding rocks is the key, because that's where the bass hang out. You have to take your time and comb the structure thoroughly. If your casts are too far apart, you could miss the spot that's holding all the fish.

When you're probing for rocks, it's important to keep your rod tip low. This maximizes what Moynagh calls the "collision factor." Stated another way, a low line angle means that the bait is more likely to collide with a rock than slide over it.

What makes a Roll'r Jig different than any other jig is the way it reacts as you inch it

Roll'r Rock Jig

Luck "E" Strike Football Jig

Yamamoto Spider Jig

Roll'r Rock Jig with weedguard

Kalin's Mop Top

A Roll'r Jig scoots ahead and kicks up silt, just like a darting crayfish.

along. When the head catches on something small, like a pebble or clam shell, the eye pivots downward when you pull on the line, causing the hook and trailer to lift up, much like a crayfish stands up with claws erect when defending itself. The Roll'r Jig's recessed eye enhances the pivoting action, because it keeps the knot pointing upward. If the knot were to slip to the front of the eye, you would lose some of the leverage required to create the kicking action.

In most cases, the jig will pull loose, move a short distance, then bump something and tip up again. But when the bait hits something solid, it hangs up. When you continue to pull, your rod loads and your line stretches. The bait then pops free and darts ahead, creating the impression of a scooting crayfish.

"When a bass grabs a Roll'r Jig," says Moynagh, "what you often feel resembles an exaggerated bluegill nibble. It doesn't feel like an aggressive strike, but it must be because a lot of the fish are hooked deep.

"Lots of times, the fish picks up the jig and swims toward you. Wind the rod tip down, hit him hard, then reel down and lean into him again. This helps sink the broad hook point.

"Don't try horsing the fish to the boat too quickly; wear them out first. The worst possible thing is that they jump just below the rod tip.

"The most common mistake in Roll'r jigging is working the bait too fast and hopping it too much. It works best when you inch it slowly along the bottom. When I hop it too much, all I catch are northern pike.

"Roll'r jigging is a super-slow technique. When you're fishing a tournament, it can be a real gut grinder. You're tempted to try a faster technique and find some hot fish. But if you stick with it, there's a good chance you'll hook some of the biggest bass in the lake."

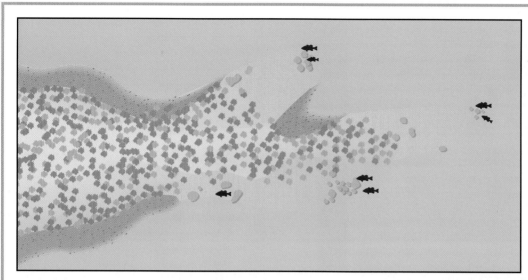

Hold your boat well off the spot you intend to fish, then make a long cast and let the bait sink to the bottom.

The position of the rock piles on this point explains why closely spaced casts are a must.

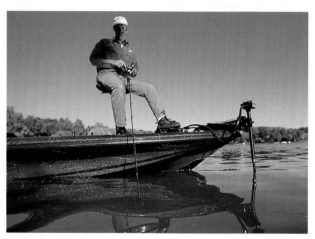

Allow the jig to rest for a few seconds, then begin inching it in. Keep your rod tip low to flatten the line angle and boost the odds that the jig will hit a rock.

As you inch the bait along, the head will catch on pebbles or other small objects on the bottom. Each time the head catches, the tail pivots upward, mimicking a crayfish assuming a defensive posture.

When the bait hangs upon something, keep reeling to "load" your rod. Suddenly the jig will pull off the snag and dart ahead, like a crayfish scooting backward to elude a predator.

When you feel a pick-up, reel down quickly to take up slack and set the hook with a hard sideways sweep of the rod. After the initial set, reel toward the fish again and "lean into" it a second time.

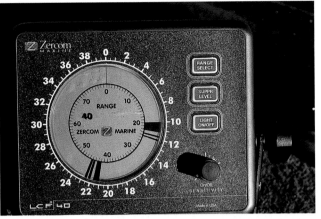

Set the gain on your depth finder so it gives you a single echo on a soft bottom (left) and a double echo on a hard bottom (right). If you set the gain too high, you'll get a double echo on both a hard and a soft bottom, so differences will be much harder to detect.

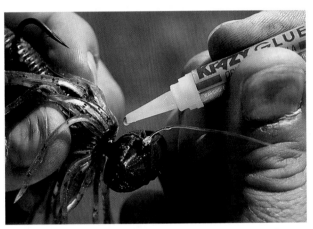

Keep a marker buoy on the deck of your boat next to your trolling motor. When you hook a fish, kick in the marker. Then, should you drift off the spot while landing the fish, you can move back quickly.

Secure the trailer with a drop of super glue to prevent it from pulling away from the jig head.

Make shorter casts and hold the rod tip higher when fishing in snaggy cover. This increases the angle between your line and the bottom, causing the jig to slide over obstructions.

Check your hook point often when fishing in the rocks and file away any rough spots that could reduce your hooking percentage. Also, check your line for nicks and retie frequently.

TUBEJIG TRICKERY

by Tim Tucker

The enthusiasm in Roland Martin's voice is still a vivid memory. The year was 1982 and Martin had recently returned from an extended fishing trip on the western desert lakes of Mead and Powell. He had made an exciting discovery and was anxious to share the news.

"I just saw the most amazing jig," Martin began. "It's made by a friend of mine, Bobby Garland, out in Utah. It's made out of plastic and the body of the jig has 30 or 40 little tentacles, so it looks like a little octopus as it falls through the water. They are throwing it in the cracks in the canyon walls and for bass they can see. It's a tremendous bait."

Years later, Martin would refer to the lure as the "finest sight-fishing bait ever made."

The lure was the Fat Gitzit, the forerunner of the tubejig that is today an integral part of any serious bass enthusiast's arsenal. It was the Gitzit that started the tubejig craze and today, despite dozens of soft-plastic copies on the market, this entire genre of fishing is referred to generically as "Gitzit fishing."

The Gitzit was born in the mind of Bobby Garland back in 1964. In the mid-1970s, the lure began to capture the imagination of his fellow western anglers who discovered its unparalleled allure in the deep, clear reservoirs where they plied their trade. But it was in the mid-1980s that the Gitzit migrated into eastern waters, where it created an entire legion of believers in waters considerably different in biological nature.

The Fat Gitzit became "The Lure That Changed the Face of Bass Fishing" in the 1980s, as light line and finesse fishing began to dominate tournament circuits from Georgia to California. Although the Gitzit was the leader of a pack of down-sized finesse lures jokingly referred to as "sissy baits," it suddenly became the answer to several fishing situations, ranging from pressured bass to clear-water sight fishing.

It was its acceptance in the East that made the Gitzit such a major-league player. And its popularity among eastern fishermen can be directly attributable to one man.

Guido Hibdon discovered the Gitzit by fishing with Garland in a tournament on Lake Mead. Garland gave him a day-long education in tubejig trickery and Hibdon came away extremely impressed and determined to apply this magical little bait to the clear waters of his home Ozark Mountains lakes – Table Rock, Bull Shoals and Lake of the Ozarks.

After proving the bait's potency to his own satisfaction, the Missouri pro demonstrated its allure to the rest of the fishing world. Most of us took notice in back-to-back national tournaments in which Hibdon's tubejigs produced 48 and 50 pounds (fourth and first places, respectively). From that point on, the Gitzit soared in popularity. And tubejigs have won too many national tournaments to count.

When & Where to Fish Tubejigs

Garland, Hibdon, Shaw Grigsby and many others have proven the versatility of the tubejig in diverse water and cover conditions, and they've shown that it's effective most any time of the year.

Bobby Garland

Bobby Garland is the inventor of the Gitzit tubejig, a finesse lure born in the canyon lakes of the West that went on to change the face of bass fishing throughout the country. His uncanny skill with light line and finesse baits made him one of the West's top tournament anglers for years. Today, Garland lives and manufactures Gitzits in Midland, Arkansas.

The wiggling tentacles of a tubejig explain its visual appeal in clear water.

"The bait catches big fish and it is a consistent producer in winter, summer, spring and fall," says Garland. "And it will catch fish in dirty water as well as clear water.

"It didn't surprise me that it would catch bass in grass lakes, which is a big reason why it caught on so well in the East. The first time I fished the prototype of this bait in a tournament, I caught my limit off a grassbed in Lake Havasu on my first five casts. Then I went into the river and began fishing some tulies (lily pads) in fairly clear water with a little color to it. I had five bass that weighed 20 pounds and then proceeded to cull every bass I had in the livewell. So I knew it could be quite effective around vegetation."

Even though you can fish a tubejig most anywhere and anytime, the bait is at its best in clear water. "I really believe the Gitzit is the best sight bait available," Garland claims. "The reason the bait works best in clear water is that the action of it often triggers a strike on the fall. When the water is a little dingy, the fish have trouble homing in on it."

Grigsby agrees that a tubejig is probably the best lure for catching visible bass. "With that bait, you can represent two major food sources of the bass," he says. "It resembles a minnow when it's floating and a crawfish once it hits the bottom, especially when you pop it and it darts backwards."

Selecting Tubejigs

Through the years, Garland developed three sizes of Gitzits for different situations. He uses a 2 1/2-, 3 3/4- or 5 1/2-inch version, depending on the prevailing size of the forage fish or the species of bass he is targeting. The smallest Gitzit is best suited for catching smallmouth and spotted bass, while largemouth will assault even the Jumbo Gitzit.

Garland most often uses the smallest Gitzit on jig heads ranging from 1/16- to 1/2-ounce in size. As a rule, he never goes heavier than 1/4-ounce in the spring and 1/2-ounce in the summer. Depth, obviously, plays a role in jig size. Garland uses the 1/16-ounce head in shallow water, 1/8-ounce in water 8 to 12 feet deep and 1/4- or 1/2-ounce in depths of 13 feet or more.

"There are exceptions," he interjects. "Sometimes in the summertime when the fish are real full from a lot of feeding, I'll use a 1/4-ounce head in shallow water to trigger a strike that I couldn't get with a slow fall. But other times, the fish want that slow fall, especially with suspended bass that may be up under a boat dock.

"I will occasionally take a 1/16-ounce lead head and cut it down real light for the times when I find fish up real shallow in moss beds or tulies or suspended under boat docks. That super-slow fall has worked quite well for me at times. But I probably fish the 1/4-ounce head on 6- to 14-pound test line most of the time."

Shaw Grigsby has won several national tournaments on the strength of a G-4 tube, which he fishes most often Texas-rigged on a size 1 to 2/0 Eagle Claw High Performance Hook with a 1/16-ounce bullet weight. Grigsby uses more weight

Popular Tubejigs

Gitzit

Luck "E" Strike
G4 Tube

Berkley
Power Tube

Riverside
Pro Tube

Tube-Rigging Options

Rig a tube on a High Performance hook, along with a bullet sinker, to make it weedless.

Substitute a Quick-Clip internal tube weight for the bullet sinker. (Lure shown in cross section.)

For light cover, rig a tube on a jig head as shown, poking the jig eye through the side of the tube.

Try skipping a tube jig to imitate a skittering shad.

Although the tubejig is most often taken during its initial descent, Garland has developed a pair of slightly unorthodox techniques for this type of finesse fishing.

"I've caught a lot of fish in the summer just by dead-sticking it," he says, "just allowing the bait to lie beneath a bush and not moving it at all. The fish will pick it up and start moving away with it, the reason being that the tails of the bait will stick up off of the bottom and wiggle. I've observed them in clear water and a lot of times a bass will get close to the bait and watch it.

"The tails are moving and he's watching it. Then when you move it a little, the bass will follow it. All of a sudden, that jig head will dig into the bottom and it will take a funny flip and the bass will inhale it.

depending on the water depth (⅛-ounce for 5 to 10 feet and ¼-ounce for deeper water). And Luck "E" Strike recently began marketing the Quick Clip, an internal tube weight designed by Grigsby. The Quick Clip eliminates the need for a bullet weight or jig head and gives the tube a more tantalizing fall.

How to Fish Tubejigs

Although the roots of the Gitzit are firmly planted in open-water structure in depths that most eastern anglers never experience, tubejigs are outstanding baits for shallow-water applications, as well.

"There are always going to be some straggler fish up shallow if you go to the right part of the lake, and these are the fish I would rather target," Garland explains. "I'll throw the bait to the edge of a bush on the shady side several feet beyond it. Keeping my rod tip high, I bring it back to the bush and then lower the rod tip to let it fall down into the shadow of the bush or rock or moss bed. That's when it will get nailed.

"If the action is slow, sometimes you need to get it down on the bottom and sort of bulldoze it along the bottom real slow."

"Another technique that has worked well for me in a tournament situation involves fishing a good ledge or point that drops off of the main channel – a place that holds a lot of fish, but these fish get pounded so much that they have wised up. In this situation, I've learned to stay back a ways and throw the Gitzit up shallow on the point and then start shaking it real hard as it comes down off of the point. That action seems to ignite a strike on fish that are heavily pressured."

A major part of tubejig trickery involves loading the lure. "A tube bait was made to have something crammed into it," Hibdon believes. "After all, it's just a hollow tube. I have put everything you can think of inside tube baits to give them a different look, sound or smell, including rattles, Alka Seltzer and visible fish attractants like SparklScales."

Knowledgeable anglers like Shaw Grigsby, Guido Hibdon, Roland Martin and others have taken Bobby Garland's simple tubejig and developed its appeal and versatility farther than he ever imagined. With their help, the tubejig has, indeed, changed the face of bass fishing.

How to Retrieve a Tubejig

Cast the bait past the shady side of a bush or other visible cover. Keeping your rod tip high, reel until the bait reaches the spot where you expect the fish are holding.

Lower your rod tip, keeping the line taut, to let the bait fall into the fish zone. This is when the fish will normally strike.

If nothing grabs the bait as it is sinking, allow it to settle to bottom and remain motionless for several seconds. Often, a fish will pick up the bait and swim off with it; be ready to set the hook.

If a fish doesn't take the motionless bait, start inching it along very slowly. The change in action will often trigger a strike.

Two Tips for Fishing Tubejigs

Insert pieces of an Alka-Seltzer tablet into the hollow body of a tubejig. The fizzing action draws attention to the bait.

Fit a tube over a jigging spoon when fishing deepwater bass. The wiggling tentacles make the spoon more attractive to bass.

SOFT PLASTICS

Carolina Rigging

A Back-to-the-Fifties Technique that's Still Winning Big

by Tim Tucker

One of the hottest techniques at all levels of bass fishing, from the national tournament circuit to backyard ponds all across America, has been Carolina-rigging soft plastics.

Born in the 1950s, Carolina-rigging has enjoyed a rebirth of sorts in the decade of the '90s as one of the dominant trends on the professional tournament scene – a fact that has filtered down to the weekend angler. Its believers say there is no better deep-water technique than the Carolina rig. And those who have learned its intricacies have found plenty of shallow-water applications for the rig as well.

Today, any bass buff worth his plastic understands the benefits of Carolina-rigging and has incorporated it into his game plan.

"I see Carolina-rigging as one of the trends of the future because it is so good for finding open-water fish," praises Florida pro Pete Thliveros. "Open-water fishing involves going out and finding new places to fish.

"The most productive way to find these places is driving along and watching your depth finder constantly. If I see some sort of irregular feature, drop-off or shallow spot, I'll stop and fish it with a Carolina rig. These places are overlooked because most fishermen go from point A to point B at 60 miles an hour. And they go over the fish. I drive slower and look for these places, which are tailor-made for the Carolina rig."

It's no wonder that Thliveros is such a big fan of the Carolina rig. Consider the pivotal role it played in three recent tournaments:

• On Tennessee's Fort Loudon Reservoir, Thliveros probed a large bay dotted with roadbeds, humps, rock piles and drop-offs with a Carolina-rigged 4-inch worm. The first bass he caught weighed about 8 pounds, and he quickly limited out while hardly moving his boat.

• While idling well offshore on North Carolina's Lake Norman, Thliveros discovered a small isolated rock pile. Again, his Carolina rig produced a trophy fish (7 pounds), followed by the rest of his limit.

• On Lake Murray in South Carolina, Thliveros avoided the crowded shorelines and limited out each day with a Carolina rig.

Pete Thliveros

Peter Thliveros is a two-time B.A.S.S. Tournament winner and six-time BASS Masters Classic qualifier who has pocketed almost half-a-million dollars in tournament earnings. Thliveros calls Jacksonville, Florida, home.

Silt stirred up by the sinker may draw the attention of a hungry bass.

shows on television. "The Texas rig drops at a constant speed dictated by the size of the worm, sinker and line. But a Carolina rig falls at sinker speed until the lead hits. Then the lizard or other bait does a little two-step, changes speed and continues down with a slower, lazier action.

"When you pull this rig up off of the bottom, the lizard comes up with a slower rise and has a totally different movement from a Texas rig on the drop. That difference in presentation can often make a big difference in your catch. Plus, you can keep the Carolina rig in one small area and make it exhibit action and movement far longer than you can a Texas rig. That ability to work it up next to cover or structure and leave it there for a while can often draw strikes when faster retrieves and other baits fail."

Dance and others also believe the clicking sound made by the heavy weight clashing with the glass bead is an attractant to bass. Some say it mimics the noise made by agitated crayfish.

For Thliveros, a Carolina rig works like a depth finder. The heavy weight helps him map out the bottom structure to a degree not possible with modern depth finders. "With any depth finder, the cone angle of the transducer is going to be so narrow that you can easily miss a 2-foot drop in 10 feet of water," he explains. "By dragging my Carolina rig, I'm like a blind man with a cane. That weight tells me everything about the bottom – if it is a hard bottom, soft bottom, shell, rocks, stumps or grass. It identifies cover like nothing I've ever used and at the same time it catches fish because it provides a subtle presentation of the bait."

One set of stumps positioned on a subtle point surrendered five bass, including three that weighed between 5 and 6 pounds.

And those are just a few of the success stories spawned by the age-old Carolina rig.

It is a lesson not lost on the top pros. Arkansas' Mark Davis, the first man to ever win the B.A.S.S. Angler of the Year and BASS Masters Classic titles in the same season, emphasizes that he spends about 20 to 30 percent of his tournament year dragging a Carolina rig.

Why Carolina Rigging?

The basic Carolina rig consists of a heavy weight (usually ¾-ounce or more), plastic or glass bead, barrel swivel, separate leader of various lengths, hook and a soft plastic lure. The heavy weight drags along the bottom, kicking up clouds of silt that simulate the activity of a crayfish. The lure trails well behind it, floating off the bottom.

"Unlike the Texas rig, the Carolina rig allows the bait to hold over the cover and gives the bass time to react to it," says Bill Dance, former tournament star and now host of one of the longest-running fishing

Rigging Up

Thliveros' Carolina rig usually consists of a 1-ounce bullet weight, glass bead and small swivel on a 17- to 20-pound-test main line. His leader, normally 14-pound clear mono,

The basic Carolina rig

ranges from 4 to 7 feet in length, depending on the height of the cover. He uses a size 1 to 2/0 hook, depending on the size of the lure.

The length of the leader is probably the most important consideration when building a Carolina rig. "Leader length is the most frequently asked question I get from people that are just getting into Carolina-rig fishing," says Mark Davis. "As a general rule, the shallower I fish, the shorter my leader. The deeper I fish, the longer the leader.

"Long leaders have their place. If I'm fishing in vegetation and want to keep my lure above the grass, I use a long leader. Another reason for a long leader is extremely clear water. If I'm fishing a spawning bed, I'll use a 7-foot leader to keep that big weight as far away from the lure as possible, to avoid spooking the bass."

Many pros, however, rarely use a leader longer than 3 feet, and some shorten their leader to as little as 10 inches when fishing around stumps.

"You can put any kind of lure and any size you want on a Carolina rig and it is going to work," says Davis. "Anything from a tiny finesse worm to a big lizard."

The undisputed favorite of Carolina-riggers (and bass) is the plastic lizard. That preference seems puzzling since bass never encounter live lizards out in the middle of the lake.

Thliveros' Carolina attractors include "French fry" baits and a variety of plastic worms. Davis relies heavily on pork baits, which he feels have a frantic, lifelike action in the water as well as a texture, taste and feel that plastic lures cannot match.

When selecting colors for Carolina-rigged lures, most pros keep it simple and base their selection primarily on water clarity. In clear water, translucent colors like cotton candy, watermelon and green-pumpkinseed seem to prevail. Off-colored conditions demand more visible colors like june bug, chartreuse and pumpkinseed with a chartreuse tail.

Carolina-Rigging Secrets

"The Carolina rig is a lot more versatile than most people realize," says Thliveros. "A lot of times, it's a search bait for me. I can put my trolling motor down and quickly either follow the contour or zig-zag back and forth to dissect the cover.

Popular Baits for Carolina Rigging

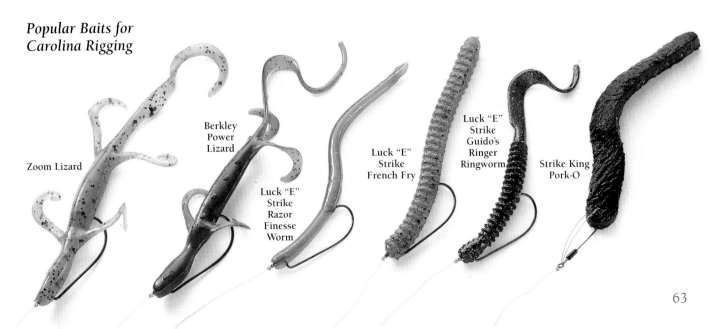

Zoom Lizard

Berkley Power Lizard

Luck "E" Strike Razor Finesse Worm

Luck "E" Strike French Fry

Luck "E" Strike Guido's Ringer Ringworm

Strike King Pork-O

The rod is arguably the most important piece of tackle involved in Carolina-rigging.

Most pros prefer a 7- to 7½-foot medium-heavy-power baitcaster, which gives you long casts and good hook-setting power. Pair this with a high-speed bait-casting reel, which helps erase slack line for long-distance hook setting, which is the norm in Carolina rigging.

Most pros prefer an abrasion-resistant monofilament for both the main line and leader. Usually, the leader is considerably smaller in diameter than the main line.

Although mono is still widely used, superlines (30- to 50-pound test) are rapidly gaining in popularity, because they telegraph strikes better and minimize the hook-setting problems that can result when the wind puts a bow in your line.

"Generally, I look for some sort of flat or deep water, maybe a deep point in over 10 feet of water. On Sam Rayburn (Reservoir), I'll throw it a lot on inside grass lines or shallow sandy areas where the bass aren't really keying in on anything in particular."

"Don't try to limit yourself with a Carolina rig," Thliveros continues. "Sure, in a situation where I am fishing deep and I can't get other baits down there, it's an absolutely great tool. But you can also throw it to shallow bedding fish."

When Carolina rigging, most pros use two basic retrieves:

"One is a very slow, steady drag with the rod tip," Thliveros explains. "The other is a slow, steady drag with intermittent jerks or fast pulls or erratic motions. When I get into an area where I feel a lot of stumps or shells, I pause it a lot and shake the rig in one spot until the fish come and get it. The best policy is to let the fish tell you what kind of retrieve to use on a given day."

"The first thing I have to see before picking up my Carolina rig is that the fish are relating to the bottom," says Mark Davis. "And if it looks like they are relating to the bottom, it must be a clean bottom – rock, shell or hard sand. I don't like throwing a Carolina rig in heavy grass or mud."

Davis claims a Carolina-rigged plastic is an excellent "back-up bait" for a crankbait, jig or Texas-rigged grub around deep structure. He has often managed to re-ignite feeding activity with a Carolina rig long after the bass stopped chasing other lures.

The Carolina rig has earned a place in the arsenal of every serious bass angler.

Thliveros lands a nice bass that took a Carolina-rigged lizard.

Six Carolina-Rigging Tips

Substitute a brass sinker and one or two glass beads for a lead sinker and plastic bead. Brass clinking against glass is much noisier than lead against plastic.

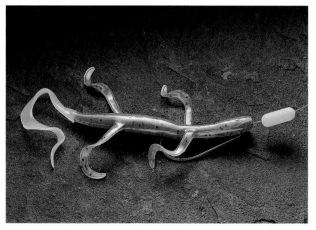

Thread a hard-foam floater onto your leader to make the bait float well off the bottom. Experiment with floats of different colors and sizes.

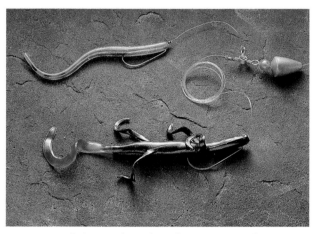

Bass commonly bite at the sinker when you're Carolina rigging. To catch these fish, rig up a trailer by substituting a three-way swivel for the barrel swivel, then tying on a 2-inch leader and a smaller bait.

Carry a supply of special dyes for coloring soft plastics. This way, when you find that the fish want a certain color, you can doctor your baits accordingly.

Make an adjustable Carolina rig by first threading on the sinker and bead and then a rubber stop . The stops come on wire rings; simply thread your line through the ring and pull

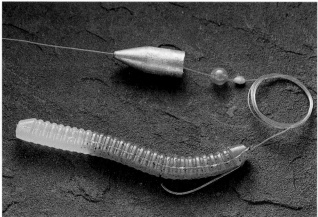

the stop onto your line (left). Next, tie on your hook and adjust the stop to make a leader of the desired length (right).

Finessing Clear-Water Bass

By Ronnie Kovach

We've all heard the old adage that 10 percent of the fishermen catch 90 percent of the fish. But when it comes to extracting largemouth bass from deep, clear, heavily pressured lakes, such as the big-bass impoundments of southern California, a more accurate estimate might be that 5 percent of the fisherman catch 95 percent of the fish.

Bass in any clear body of water are naturally more wary than their murky-water cousins, but when you're dealing with Florida-strain largemouths in lakes swarming with recreational boaters, the fish are even more leery of any offering that does not look real.

Western bass anglers have long understood the need for realism in their presentation and have relied heavily on lifelike soft-plastic baits. Some anglers began experimenting with giant soft plastics that resembled the rainbow trout that are stocked in many western lakes. Others opted for a more subtle approach, downsizing their baits and using very light line to tempt the finicky biters. The latter method has been dubbed "finesse fishing."

Finesse fishermen use a simple variation of the Carolina rig. It consists of a lead split-shot crimped a foot or two above a small Texas-hooked soft-plastic lure. Most anglers use 6- to 8-pound-test monofilament for an ultra-natural presentation.

It's easy to understand why this tactic has been so effective in the West and now in other regions. Not only does the lighter line draw more strikes in clear water, it allows the tiny 2- to 4-inch plastic worm to "swim" more naturally on a retrieve than does heavier line. The minuscule lures mimic the 3- to 4-inch long shad and crayfish found in these impoundments. As the split shot bumps bottom, it causes the bait to rise and fall, imitating the natural movements of these two major forage items.

Finesse fishing with a split-shot rig is the ultimate "slow-down" presentation. Bass pros from the South originally had a hard time understanding how any sensible angler could spend several minutes on a single retrieve. But as they learned more about the technique, it soon became obvious that it worked magic on many ultra-clear waters that had a long-standing reputation for tough fishing.

The pros also were quick to discover that finesse fishing was the answer on many heavily fished waters that had been bombarded with practically every type of bait imaginable. Fish that had become almost immune to the usual offerings could often be enticed into grabbing a tiny soft-plastic snack.

Today, finesse fishing has caught on throughout the country and is a part of every professional bass angler's repertoire.

Best Conditions for Finesse Fishing

Finesse fishing works best in deep, clear lakes with a minimum of aquatic vegetation or woody cover. The small baits are not as likely to draw the attention of bass in dense-cover situations.

Because the baits are weighted so lightly, the technique is most effective in shallow water. It is not recommended at depths exceeding 20 feet.

Finesse fishing works well from spring through fall and at most any time of the day. It excels under conditions that normally slow bass-fishing action, such as sunny skies and cold fronts. It is also one of the best options during the dreaded post-spawn "recuperation" period.

But it is not a good choice in windy weather. When a gust catches your line, it lifts the light weight off the bottom and causes you to lose your "feel."

Finesse fishing is ideal for thoroughly covering small pieces of structure or cover, such as a rock pile or brush clump, where you expect bass to be holding. But, because the

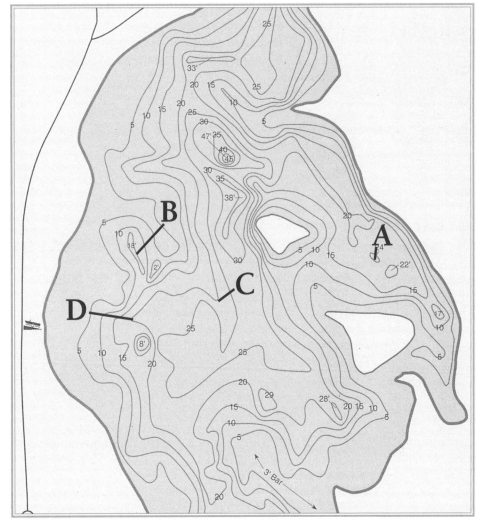

Finesse fishing is the ideal technique for working small, distinct pieces of structure such as (**A**) a small hump, (**B**) a slender rock reef, (**C**) the sharp tip of an extended point, and (**D**) a sharp inside turn in the breakline.

presentation is so slow and painstaking, it is not the best way to cover large expanses of unfamiliar structure. There, you can locate fish more quickly by using a fast presentation, like spinnerbaiting or crankbaiting.

Rigging Up for Finesse Fishing

Almost any small soft-plastic bait that measures 4 inches or less in length can be used for finesse fishing. Tiny, straight-tailed plastic worms, often called "weenie worms," are one of the most popular baits, although some anglers prefer paddle-tail eels, curly-tail grubs or crayfish imitations.

The bait is normally rigged on a size 1 or 2 light-wire worm hook. A single round split-shot is pinched onto the line about 12 to 24 inches above the bait. Be sure to use round, rather than winged, split-shot; the wings tend to hang up on the bottom and interfere with your feel.

How to Make a Tandem-Hook Finesse Rig

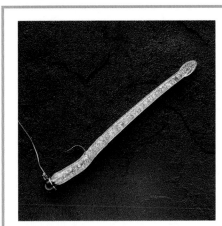

1 Thread a small soft-plastic bait onto a ¹⁄₁₆- to ¹⁄₈-ounce jig head.

2 Tie a short length of 12-pound mono onto the bend of your jig hook. Then tie on a worm hook the same size as the jig hook.

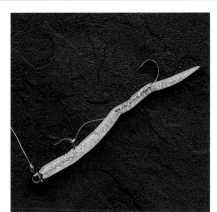

3 Thread the worm onto the trailer, leaving the hook point exposed.

Soft Plastics / Finessing Clear-Water Bass

Popular Finesse Baits

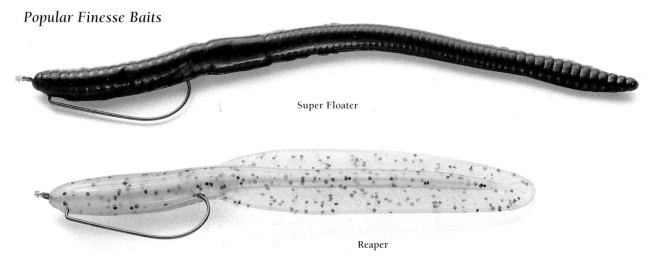

Super Floater

Reaper

In windy weather, you may want to substitute a $\frac{1}{16}$- to $\frac{1}{8}$-ounce bullet sinker for the split-shot. But you'll have to peg the sinker to your line to maintain good feel.

Another variation on the basic split-shot rig is the tandem-hook rig. Intended to catch short strikers, the rig is gaining popularity among West Coast tournament anglers.

Finesse-Fishing Techniques

Finesse fishermen use three basic presentations: stitching, dead-baiting and doodlin'.

Mike Folkestad of Yorba Linda, California is regarded as one of the top finesse fishermen on the West Coast. Folkestad will key in on a particular piece of structure, meticulously presenting his worm at all possible angles to cover every spot where bass may be holding. To do this, he makes repeated casts, "stitching" the bait back to the boat with an ultra-slow retrieve.

Folkestad picks up the line in his left hand, then pulls it in 6 to 18 inches before winding up the slack. As he winds, the worm rests motionless on the bottom. He continues stitching until the worm reaches the boat. It may take 10 minutes for a single retrieve.

Lunker Floridas are extremely tempermental fish. They rarely respond to quick-moving lures. Slow-crawling crawdads make up a good share of their diet. This explains the astounding effectiveness of the stitching retrieve for catching record-class largemouths.

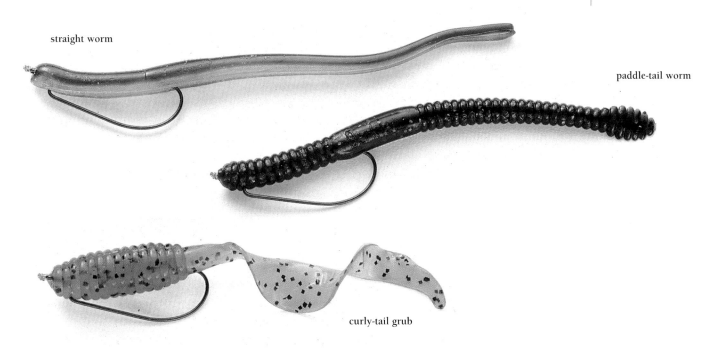

straight worm

paddle-tail worm

curly-tail grub

Stitching enables you to feel even the lightest bite.

patience, but this tactic works amazingly well, particularly on lethargic cold-water bass.

The doodlin' technique has also received considerable fanfare of late. Doodlin' means fishing vertically, shaking your rod tip to to make the bait dance erratically. Although doodlin' is normally done in deep water, particularly in winter, many western pros now use the doodlin' technique year-round, in water of most any depth.

The rig is fairly simple. Designed by trophy bass expert Don Iovino of Burbank, California, the basic doodlin' set up consists of a 3- to 4-inch straight or paddle-tail worm. The worm is rigged Texas-style behind a $3/16$- ounce bullet sinker. Between the bullet weight and the worm is a brightly colored faceted glass bead. Iovino emphasizes that the bead must be faceted in order to refract light erratically underwater. It must also be made of glass rather than plastic. Glass makes a louder "clacking" noise, calling in hook-shy bass to investigate as it bumps against the sinker.

Iovino not only doodles along deep ledges, but also around shoreline targets such as boat docks, piers, submerged brush, rock piles, rocky dam faces and clay cliffs. "I've doodled all over the county, Iovino says, "in five feet of water or 50 feet of water – dirty water or clear water." For doodlin' at depths of 10 feet or less, he uses a $1/16$- to $1/8$-ounce bullet sinker.

Sometimes, the doodlin' and stitching techniques are combined to fish shallower targets. "Doodle-stitching" involves casting the bait out and retrieving it by pulling in the line with one hand while shaking the rod with the other. Between pulls, pause and shake the bait in place. Doodle-stitching may draw the attention of bass that ignore a plain stitching retrieve.

These finesse-fishing methods are starting to catch on in clear lakes throughout the country. Try them; they might just open up a whole new world of fishing on waters you gave up on years ago.

Recently, western anglers have taken this slow-down technique to the extreme. With their new method, called "dead baiting," they intentionally make long pauses during the retrieve. Sometimes the pauses last for well over a minute.

The trick is to use a high-buoyancy worm, such as the Super Floater, that will float well off the bottom during the pauses. This rather bland-looking worm, which has air bubbles injected into the plastic, has become the "secret weapon" of western bass anglers who use the dead-bait routine.

Accomplished dead-baiters retrieve very slowly until they feel the "tick" signalling that a bass has nipped the worm. Then the waiting game begins. As the Super Floater rests suspended in the water, the bass keep an eye on it and eventually hit it with a vengeance. It takes nerve-wracking

This cross-section of the Super Floater shows that it is impregnated with air bubbles.

Soft Plastics / Finessing Clear-Water Bass

Finicky bass can't resist a doodled worm.

Two Finesse-Fishing Tips

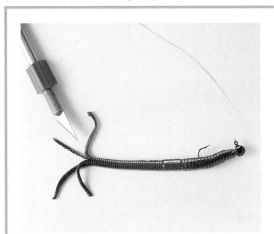

Customize the Super Floater by carefully slicing the tail into four thin sections so the worm appears to have "tentacles". These will flair out as the bait rests and seductively pulsate as you jig it.

To make the hook point penetrate the plastic more easily on the hook set, bore a cavity in the grub using a tool called the "Grub-gutter," available in western tackle shops. You can also put a float or worm rattle in the cavity.

The Other Extreme: Magnum Soft Plastics

Although finesse baits account for a good number of giant western bass, trophy hunters know that the big fish are lazy – there are times when they would rather eat one big mouthful than a dozen small bites.

In recent years, trophy specialists have been been tallying impressive numbers of giant bass on magnum soft-plastic baits made to replicate planted rainbow trout – a favorite morsel for double-digit Florida-strain largemouths. Many of these baits are nearly a foot long, and a few measure up to 18 inches in length. These baits not only catch lunker bass, but anglers are finding that there are times when they work better than smaller lures for average-sized bass.

Savvy western anglers have long known about the effectiveness of magnum soft plastics. The problem was finding them. Very few were being manufactured, so serious big-bass addicts had to mold their own.

Today, several manufacturers are producing these huge baits. Here is a review of some of the more popular magnum soft plastics currently being used on western waters.

Trout Imitations

These are the best-known giant soft-plastic lures in the West. Most of the imitation trout are hand-poured by such manufacturers as A.A. Worms and Worm King. You can cast or slow-troll them on a heavy baitcasting outfit with 15- to 20-pound mono, but some anglers prefer to troll them with lead-core line to reach big bass suspended in deep water.

These 6- to 10-inch-plus baits are most often rigged on a $3/8$- to 1-ounce leadhead with an open hook, but there are some other rigging options. A.A. Worms markets a special harness with a pair of treble hooks and a metal diving lip that inserts into the soft plastic. This permits the angler to slowly retrieve or troll the giant bait a few feet under the surface. The rear "stinger" hook also helps stick many of the short biters.

Optimum Swim Baits actually molds the lead head into the body of their soft-plastic rainbow trout and giant shiner minnows. This creates a "soft-head" lure with no metal head for the fish to feel and reject.

Giant Slugs

Soft-plastic slugs have been the rage across the country in recent years. Out West, you can now buy hand-poured versions that exceed 12 inches in length.

These baits are rigged on a long-shank, 5/0 hook, using the same hooking method employed for the 3- to 6-inch slugs. But unlike the smaller versions, which are normally twitched in shallow water, giant slugs are designed primarily as deep-water baits.

In big-bass waters stocked with trout, trophy hunters slowly drag rainbow trout-colored slugs on Carolina rigs over submerged humps and along deep ledges.

Snakes

Although southern bass fishermen have been throwing 10- to 18-inch worms or "snakes" for years, only a handful of western anglers have relied on these lures. Mike Folkestad, one of the top touring pros in the West, fishes the big worms on the legendary San Diego-area lakes. "I'm usually looking for a big fish at places like Hodges, San Vincente, or Otay," says Folkestad. "A 9- to 12-inch worm is my primary bait. What continues to amaze me is how smaller 2- to 3-pounders inhale these big baits."

Folkestad is extremely meticulous in fishing the "snakes". With a large 4/0 to 5/0 worm hook, he Texas-rigs the long baits but uses only a $1/8$- ounce worm weight. He points out that

Popular Giant Soft-Plastics

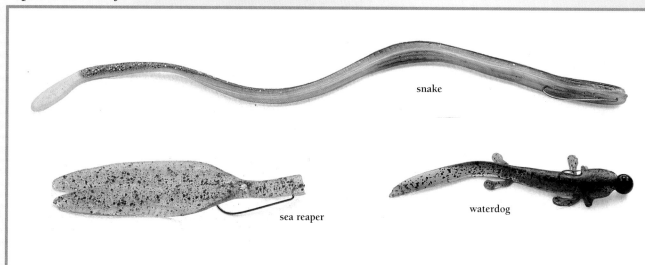

snake

sea reaper

waterdog

"Floridas in these small lakes are very touchy. They will strike the big worms at the head. But it is important not to have much resistance when the fish starts to move off with the worm. That's why I prefer to use the smallest worm weight possible.

"I also use a new snake from Anglers' Choice. I helped design it with a pre-grooved hook channel that allows for instant penetration. This is critical when using big worms with extra thick bodies."

Magnum Grubs

It is common knowledge that many western bass tournaments are won by anglers split-shotting 2- to 3-inch curly-tail grubs. A recent spin on this technique is to upscale dramatically and split-shot longer 6-inch models. The Berkley Magnum Power Grub along with Kalin's Mogumbo were designed for saltwater species. However, on big Western lakes like Mead, Mohave, and Havasu, these magnum curly-tails replicate anything from large shad and shiners to small bluegills and crappies, and will catch bass year-round.

You can fish the oversize grubs many different ways. Rig them Texas-style and flip them into dense cover, swim them like a crankbait on a $1/8$- to $1/2$-ounce lead head or rig them Carolina-style and crawl them along in deep water.

Giant Eels

Plastic eels were popular in Southern California in the early 1960's, but they were soon replaced by the smaller hand-poured finesse worms. Some hand-pour companies are now marketing a giant version of these eels, measuring almost 11 inches in length. Most commonly, these eels are sold in rainbow trout finish and made to lazily float above the bottom.

The majority of eel fishermen prefer to Carolina-rig the big baits. A $3/4$- to 1-ounce sliding egg sinker will take the eel down to depths of more than 60 feet.

Use a 5/0 to 6/0 worm hook when Texas-rigging the giant eel for the Carolina set-up. Be patient and give the fish some time to thoroughly mouth this extra-long bait.

Waterdogs

It's no secret that one of the most effective of all live baits for bass is the "waterdog," which is the larval stage of the tiger salamander.

Both Anglers Choice and A.A. Worms hand-pour lifelike replicas of this amphibian. The soft-plastic waterdogs are almost seven inches long and are fairly thick through the body and the tail.

Western guide Troy Folkestad, a renowned big fish expert, catches giant bass on these baits simply by inching them along the bottom. Not only do trophy-class bass attack this bait, but you'll catch a lot of 2 to 3 pound "keepers." Fish the plastic waterdog on a $1/4$- to $3/8$- ounce open-hook jig, or rig it Texas-style and drag it along the bottom.

Sea Reapers

Most West Coast bass fishermen will attest to the potency of tiny 2- to 3-inch reapers on deep, clear impoundments. These miniature leech-like baits are made to mimic the threadfin shad found in these lakes.

Mike Leopold, a former professional bass guide and now an instructor with the Eagle Claw Saltwater Fishing Schools, worked with the experts at A.A. Worms to develop a huge, magnum-class "Sea Reaper". "Initially, I designed this palm-size reaper to catch halibut on the drift off the California coast. What I did not anticipate was how effective the Sea Reaper would be on largemouth bass," says Leopold.

Interestingly, the big reaper works well not only on a Carolina rig, but also when fished totally weightless with a Texas-style setup. "I use a 5/0 worm hook," notes Leopold, "and then cast into the shallows without any additional weight. At night, especially under moonlit conditions, bass of all sizes home in on the bait as it falls like a big shad or small crappie. During the day, it is highly effective Carolina-rigged and dragged through weedbeds."

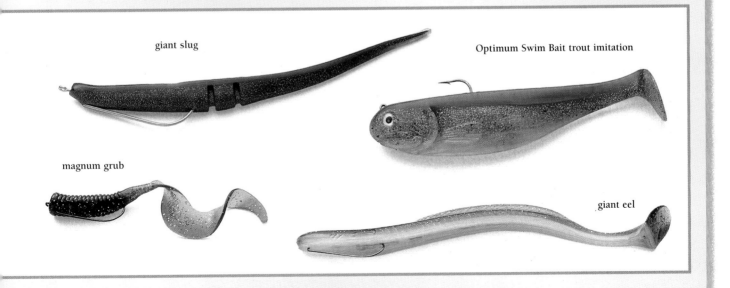

giant slug

Optimum Swim Bait trout imitation

magnum grub

giant eel

The Science of Sight-Fishing

by Tim Tucker

The excitement in Shaw Grigsby's voice was undeniable. "How would you like to photograph a giant bass tomorrow? I mean a giant," the Florida pro exclaimed over about 50 miles of telephone lines. "I've found a huge female, but I couldn't catch her today. I ran out of light, but I know I'll catch her tomorrow."

The former eight-time national tournament champion had just spent a day on his favorite spring-fed river, taking advantage of the full moon and its effect on big female spawning bass. The conditions were perfect for his favorite style of fishing – bright, sunny skies and calm. And the bass were locked onto their spawning beds.

Grigsby had spotted a huge bass positioned atop a well-hidden bed in the midst of a patch of lily pads. After watching the bass and its male companion for a while, he sensed that the female was in the process of depositing her eggs on the nest. Few anglers know more about the spawning habits of bass than Grigsby, who opted to leave her alone.

When we returned the next day, the monstrous bass was still around the bed, but her egg-laying duties had been completed. So Grigsby began a systematic approach designed to coax her into striking.

It is often necessary to catch the male bass before the female can be caught. In this case, it took nearly two hours to hook the male. Then, Grigsby immediately cast a small plastic tubejig to the female, who inhaled it. A frantic battle ensued through the dense stalks of the pads before he was able to get a firm grip on the enormous bass.

A conservationist at heart, Grigsby had the male bass released onto the bed before he even took time to admire his big female mate. Returning the male to the bed ensured that the eggs would not go unguarded, he explained.

The impressive specimen measured 27½ inches in length and weighed exactly 13½

pounds – the biggest bass ever caught by the talented pro and one of the largest fish documented in central Florida in years. After a few photos and a brief rest in a livewell bath of protective chemicals, Grigsby proudly released her.

She swam briskly back to her nest, no worse for the battle. And Grigsby seemed almost as pleased about the healthy release of this big breeder as he had been when he caught her.

Grigsby is America's premier sight fisherman, the king of a growing legion of anglers who have mastered the intricacies involved in fooling wary clear-water bass. Over the past few years, sight fishermen have become a force to contend with on the pro bass fishing circuit.

"Everybody assumes sight fishing means bed fishing, but that's far from the truth," emphasizes Missouri pro Guido Hibdon, the father of sight fishing in the East. "We sight-fish 12 months out of the year, and most of the time the spawning season is long gone.

"For some guys, sight fishing is like year-round hunting. We travel around the country and actually hunt down those visible

Shaw Grigsby

Shaw Grigsby is an eight-time national tournament champion who has qualified for the prestigious BASS Masters Classic on eight occasions. One of five pros to pass the $1 million mark in tournament earnings, he is also the host of the popular television show, "One More Cast with Shaw Grigsby," on The Nashville Network. Grigsby lives in Gainesville, Florida.

Stand in the bow and move along at a slow but constant speed with your trolling motor, looking for fish or the movements or shadows that indicate fish. Be sure to wear drab clothing, wear polarized sunglasses and keep the sun at your back as much as possible to minimize glare. Try to keep a low profile, keep body movement to a minimum and avoid making any noise.

bass in lakes everywhere. You had better know something about this type of fishing or you are going to really lose out."

What You See is What You Get

When it comes to sight fishing, Grigsby has the vision of a diamond-cutter. His ability to detect the movement of a fin, a shadow protruding from a bush or when a bass has eaten his tubejig is amazing.

"The number-one factor with sight fishing, obviously, is vision," he says. "A lot of people can see well, but they don't realize what they are looking at. That all comes with experience."

Visible bass are available throughout the year, he reminds us. Clear-water areas can be found on most lakes and reservoirs, and a portion of the bass population will be shallow at all times. The first step in sight fishing is knowing how and where to look.

High-Percentage Sight-Fishing Targets
by Rich Zaleski

This diagram depicts a typical spawning cove. Included is a selection of spots that you can't afford not to fish, even if you don't see a bass on a bed.

A – Beneath the overhanging branches of a partially submerged fallen tree. There's almost always a bed in a spot like this. Perhaps the broken light patterns from the branches provide camouflage and aid bass in protecting the nest. Or maybe the fish just like to get into places that are difficult to cast to. Whatever the reason, it's a high-percentage target of the first magnitude.

B – Stump in shallow water. Bass love to bed alongside a stump on a point or in a shallow cove. This one's a no-brainer.

C – Transition where steep (but not too deep) bank meets flatter taper of point. There's almost surely a bed or two in there somewhere, but even if there isn't, it's exactly the kind of spot a big female is likely to hole up.

D – Deep stump. Depending on water clarity and how late into the spawning season it is, a stump in five feet or more of water might have a bed tucked in next to it. But more likely, it might have a bed right smack on top of it. That's doubly true if there are spotted bass in the lake.

E – Point at the mouth of a side cut. This may well be the best spot in the entire cove. The steepest break from a flat, firm-bottom nesting area

into a channel is right there, and that channel leads into protected waters. This could be where most of the fish that spawn in the cove hesitate for a while on their way in and out.

F - Deep dock. This is always a good target, especially if the end of the dock is a floating section with anchors.

G – Dock section on narrow shoreline shelf along steep bank. If there are any bass bedding on the shelf, you can bet that there will be at least one bed partially under that dock. The corner where the dock meets the bank on the more protected side is the spot most likely to hold fish.

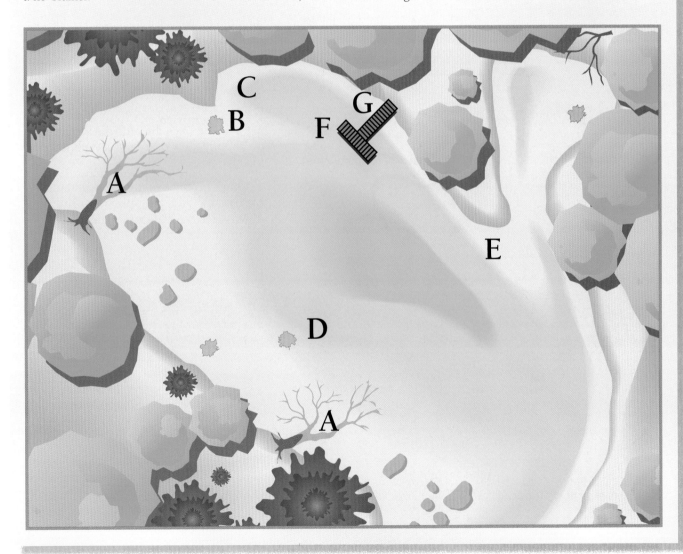

Storm Jr. Thunderstick

Rebel Pop-R

Blue Fox
Super
Vibrax

Luck "E" Strike
G4 Tube

Culprit Jerkworm

Culprit Wienee Worm

Luck "E" Strike Guido Bug

Jawtek Wacky Craw

How Grigsby Rigs a Tube

"It is the same as normal fishing in that you are trying to pinpoint what is holding the fish – the difference is that you are doing it visually rather than with a lure," he explains. "My best advice is to put the trolling motor down, get shallow and learn what to look for.

"I scan from the bank out to about as far as I can see. And that's it. I'm not going to try to look in 5 feet of water if I only have 2 feet of visibility. I'm going to look in that zero to 2-foot range where I can see the bottom or see well below the surface. I'll put my boat just inside that zone and scan that area from the shore to where my boat is."

Lures for Sight Fishing

Day in and day out, Grigsby's most productive sight-fishing lure is a Luck 'E' Strike G-4 tube rigged with a size 1 or 1/0 Eagle Claw High Performance Hook (which he designed especially for tube fishing) and a ¹⁄₁₆- or ¹⁄₈-ounce bullet weight. Or, he may rig the tube with a Quick Clip (p.55), an internal tube weight that he designed to ride on the hook shaft inside the lure.

He sometimes discards the weight to get a painfully slow descent that might tempt inactive bass.

Other productive lures for catching visible bass include small plastic worms, a down-sized jig-and-pork combination, floating minnowbaits, in-line spinners and noisy topwater chuggers.

1 Push the High Performance hook through the nose of the bait and out the side, as shown.

2 Give the hook a half turn, push it through up to the eye, then attach the wire clip to the shank. This prevents the tube from slipping back on the hook.

3 Push the hook through the bottom of the tube and out the top so the point just barely protrudes.

How to Catch Bass You've Sighted

It's easy to spot bass, but getting them to bite is another story. Many of the bass you see will be skittish and not interested in your bait. To be successful at sight fishing, you must know how to visually determine if a bass is catchable. Here are some things to look for.

"The way a fish handles itself with a cast will tell you a lot," Grigsby says. "If it spooks immediately, you know that it is a skittish fish and you may as well forget about it. If you make a good cast and the fish doesn't spook, you know you've got a good shot at catching it. He's probably pretty aggressive and is hunting for food. You can tell all that by his initial movement when you make a cast.

"After that, you're looking for little details about the fish, feedback that you can utilize to catch that fish—if he moves toward the bait or is lying back away from it. If he doesn't really seem to want to come to it, maybe you need to change the bait. Watch how he moves toward the bait and see if he gets excited or looks agitated, which you can tell by fin or tail movements that will get real frantic.

"If the fish does a nose-dive on your bait, you know he's about to bite it. Any of those movements are very aggressive and if the fish doesn't bite at that point, you've messed up somehow. You did a wrong movement with the bait.

A bass that moves aggressively toward your lure or stares at it with fins erect is highly catchable.

A bass that scurries off at the sight of your lure or shows no reaction and maintains its resting attitude will be nearly impossible to catch.

Skip cast, using a sidearm motion, to place your lure several feet ahead of a swimming bass. A skip cast works better than a regular cast, because the skipping bait imitates a skittering baitfish.

"All fish are different and sometimes you have to let the tube sit totally still to get a bite. If moving the bait brings no reaction, you need to let it sit still. You want him to react positively to it. He needs to either close the distance between him and the bait or make some gesture of aggressiveness."

If you try to approach a cruising or spawning bass, you'll probably scare it away. The best approach is to stay well away from it and make long casts. The exception is when you can get a piece of cover, such as an overhanging tree limb, between you and the fish. Then, you can get close enough to easily observe the fish's actions while using the cover as a shield.

If you find a bedding bass, you can often aggravate it into striking. This usually involves first catching (and tanking) the male bass and making repetitive casts onto the bed to provoke the female guardian. Reaction time, casting accuracy and speed are critical as you search for the exact part of the white, oval-shaped bed that the bass is zealously guarding.

If you spot a bass cruising down a bank or swimming around some object, you have to devise a strategy for intercepting its movement. After judging the direction that

Always wear polarized sunglasses when sight fishing. The photos above show unpolarized (left) and polarized (right) views of the same fish. As a rule, brown-tinted lenses work best under sunny skies; yellow-tinted, when it's cloudy.

Use a fluorocarbon leader to minimize line visibility. Fluorocarbon has the same light-refraction properties as water, making it less visible than monofilament.

Try not to spook fish with your shadow. There is always a delicate balancing act in keeping the sun at your back to reduce glare and, at the same time, keeping your shadow off the fish.

the fish is heading, try to move ahead of it. Cast well in front of the fish and time your retrieve to intercept the fish as far ahead as possible. This way, the fish will be approaching a lure that is already in place, rather than one that has just splashed down.

Once the bass gets close to the lure, don't pop it or make a lot of commotion with it – just barely move it.

Sight fishing has become an important part of the arsenal of both tournament pros and weekend anglers. With the proper approach and mindset, you don't have to feel intimidated at the thought of casting to visible bass.

Fishing for Bedding Smallmouth

Terry Baksay, a tournament pro from Connecticut, says, "Smallmouth are much easier to catch off a bed than largemouth. You can park your boat right over a smallie's bed and drop a tube bait or a grub in front of him and he's going to bite it eventually. You almost can't spook him off the bed, and even when you do, if you just sit there a minute or two, he'll be back and ready to bite."

Soft Jerkbaits

Big Trouble for Anglers ... And Bass

by Don Wirth

You've probably read about soft-plastic jerkbaits being among the hottest lures on the professional bass-fishing circuit. Maybe you've even bought and fished some of these baits. And if you did, chances are your results have been less than spectacular. Bass haven't jumped all over the lure, you've had trouble casting the baits long distances and setting the hook – and that line twist!

If soft-plastic jerkbaits have got you confused and frustrated, you're not alone, says Tennessee bass tournament veteran Charlie Ingram (Bio p.97). In his talks with anglers around the country, a topic that invariably comes up is how to fish soft jerkbaits.

"They aren't like other artificials," Ingram says. "And that's one reason people have so much trouble getting the hang of them. Relating rigging techniques and retrieves used with other kinds of lures to soft jerkbaits will only lead to trouble."

When fishing soft jerkbaits, weekend anglers fail to rig the baits properly and make the mistake of overfishing them, Ingram says. He made the same mistake himself when he first started fishing soft jerkbaits, he now admits. He jerked them "too hard, too fast and too often," trying to impart way too much action to the bait.

Ingram says the advantage of soft jerkbaits like the Slug–Go is that they sink very slowly and resemble a dying baitfish. He gets 90 percent of his strikes when the bait moves horizontally. This, in itself, goes "against the grain" of anglers who spend a lot of time fishing worms, grubs and other head–weighted soft–plastic lures. But, he insists, soft jerkbaits are not plastic worms; they are meant to give a horizontal, not vertical, presentation to the fish. He says it took some practice before he understood how to work these lures properly.

"The term jerkbait is a misnomer because you shouldn't jerk these lures at all," Ingram says. "Instead, develop a rhythm with the bait, alternating soft twitches and pulls with time for the bait to settle slowly. Jerking the bait simply is not a realistic presentation."

Ingram discovered early that the subtle twitch-pull-rest retrieve needed to make bass respond to a soft jerkbait is difficult to grasp. The lure doesn't throb, rattle or vibrate; it's a dart-and-settle lure. His best retrieve is "a twitch and pull" at the same time. This subtle rod movement causes the bait "to glide upward, then arch back down slowly—a super-realistic presentation."

Rigging soft jerkbaits improperly results in missed fish, twisted line and poor lure action, according to Ingram. You must rig the hook absolutely straight. If it's off to one side or otherwise off kilter, what then? The bait won't perform well and line twist will triple.

On the pages that follow, Ingram reveals his tricks for rigging and fishing soft-plastic jerkbaits to NAFC Members.

Selecting & Rigging Soft Jerkbaits

The main consideration in selecting the right soft jerkbait is size. Six-inch models are, by far, the most popular. But smaller sizes come in handy when the bass are highly pressured or in a negative mood. In a typical tournament, Ingram usually starts with the 6-inch jerkbait, but he often switches to the 3-inch model when the bite slows down. Ingram calls the 3-inch soft jerkbait "a great finesse lure."

Soft jerkbaits lures come in every color imaginable, but Ingram sticks to basic shad colors. His favorite is the Arkansas Shiner, which has a brown back and pearl sides. Ingram says it will catch fish anywhere in the country.

Rigging a soft jerkbait properly is as important as retrieving it correctly. On the

For best results, a soft jerkbait should sink horizontally.

6-inch lure, for example, Ingram uses a size 5/0 offset worm hook, and on the 3-inch version, the same hook in size 1/0. Using a hook that's too small will mean lost fish, he says. The hook can't penetrate through the plastic and into the jaw of the bass. Using a hook that's too large will result in decreased lure action.

Ingram rigs a soft jerkbait by first inserting the point of the hook ⅛ inch into the nose of the lure, then bringing it out and reinserting the point through the bait's belly—as when Texas-rigging a plastic worm. But with a soft jerkbait, the hook point is normally left exposed. "The point will rest in the concave back of the worm," Ingram explains. "If I'm fishing in cover, I'll keep the hook point very close to the lure's back. If I'm fishing open water, I'll run the point way out."

Ingram nabs short strikers by adding a "stinger" hook (opposite). But a stinger is not recommended in situations where the exposed treble hook would snag up or foul in weeds.

Ingram often inserts a weight when the fish aren't coming up for the lure, or when it's windy and he's having trouble casting it. The weight also helps prevent the wind from putting a bow in your line and pulling the bait to the surface. By sticking the weight in the midsection of the bait, it will maintain its horizontal fall.

How to Rig a Soft Jerkbait

1 Push the point of an offset hook into the bait about ⅛ inch and then bring it out the bottom. Pull the hook into the plastic until the eye barely protrudes.

2 Hold the hook alongside the bait, note the position of the rear of the bend (dotted line) then push the hook upward through the center of the body, following this line. This way, the bait will ride straight.

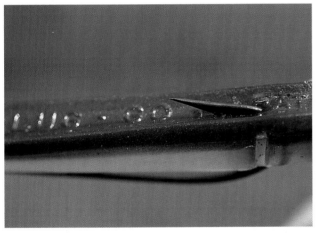

3 The hook point should rest in the groove on the back of the bait. How much the point is exposed depends on the density of the cover.

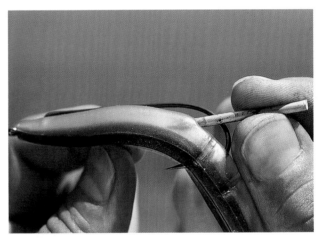

4 For extra depth or windy weather, insert a special lead weight or a small nail into the belly of the bait just in front of the hook bend.

How to Rig a Stinger on a Soft Jerkbait

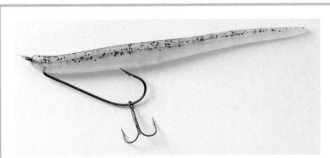

1 Slide a size 4 treble hook over the main hook before pushing it into the worm.

2 Push one point of the treble into the worm, as shown. Or, simply let the hook dangle.

Recommended Tackle

The proper tackle for fishing soft jerkbaits is mandatory, Ingram points out. The wrong rod will lead to "missed fish, short casts and needless frustration"

Ingram fishes the 6-inch bait on a 6-foot, medium-heavy-power baitcasting rod, which gives him plenty of tip snap for casting long distances and enough power to drive the hook through the plastic and into the fish's jaw.

Ingram uses a wide-spool baitcasting reel that doesn't have anti-backlash magnets. Long casts are necessary when fishing a soft jerkbait in clear water, and he believes the magnets reduce casting distance.

Ingram uses mono of at least 14-pound test when using a 6-inch bait and, around heavy cover, he switches to 17- to 30-pound line, even in gin-clear water. "Heavy line isn't going to hurt," he maintains, "because fish key in on the lure so much."

Fishing Soft Jerkbaits

Soft jerkbaits prove their value on most major tournament circuits, Ingram notes. He especially likes to fish them in the spring, when the water temperature climbs into the upper 60s.

"The bait works great after the spawn on a clear lake," Ingram says. "You can fish it over the top by walking the dog or skipping it over the surface, then allowing it to settle. They'll jump all over it when they won't hit a topwater lure."

But bigger fish may be reluctant to come up to take the bait within the top layer of water, so Ingram lets it sink until he can just barely see it. "The fish can see you," he maintains, "so they won't move up to take the bait. But if you wear polarized glasses and keep your eyes on the lure, you can often see fish strike."

If visibility conditions are not ideal, however, you may have to rely on watching the line instead of the lure. If it moves off, set the hook.

Angle your rod tip downward and retrieve with short twitches and pauses to achieve a "walk-the-dog" action.

Four Tips for Fishing Soft Jerkbaits

Rig a soft jerkbait so the head is turned slightly upward, as shown. This gives the bait a slightly different action, causing it to glide upward when you twitch and slowly sink when you pause.

If desired, push a plastic "keeper" over the point of the main hook to prevent it from pulling back into the bait. Make the discs from a coffee can lid, using a paper punch.

Lay soft jerkbaits into a tackle box with long trays and be sure they're perfectly straight. If they're stored with a bend, you won't be able to straighten them and they won't run true.

Avoid casting a soft jerkbait crosswind. The wind will put a bow in your line and drag the bait to the surface. Casting with the wind minimizes the dragging problem and also reduces backlashing.

Ingram retrieves a soft jerkbait with his rod tip close to the water. When he detects a strike, he sets the hook to the side, not upwards. This gives him more power.

With the 3-inch lure and light line, he winds up slack and "just tightens up" to set the hook; the needle-sharp point of the fine-wire hook will penetrate easily. He's careful not to set the hook immediately. He lets the fish turn before he sets to prevent pulling the bait away from the bass.

If a bass swirls at a 6-inch jerkbait but refuses to strike, Ingram will immediately cast a 3-incher to the same spot.

Besides fishing the lures shallow, he'll move offshore when bass are suspended or schooling around steep-sloping banks or points.

When working deep structure, Ingram sometimes fishes a soft jerkbait on a Carolina rig. It allows him to cover a lot of water quickly and present the lure realistically to the bass.

Many fishermen give soft-plastic jerkbaits a try, but they don't find immediate success and soon give up on them. If you're in this category, take Charlie Ingram's advice: "Use the proper tackle, rig 'em correctly, don't overfish 'em and don't be too quick to set the hook. Soft jerkbaits will catch limit after limit of bass when you work 'em right."

Speed Wormin'

by Tim Tucker

It is a typical Okeechobee spring day, sunny and bright. But this day has not been typical in the respect that the bass population in this famous southern-Florida hotspot just isn't cooperating.

As a guide and tournament angler, Larry Lazoen knows the 730-square-mile lake as well as most people know their back yard. Yet, the shallow, weedy waters of Okeechobee have held him hostage on this still morning, refusing to yield any of its aquatic bounty despite the repeated offerings of a plastic worm, weedless spoon and crankbait.

Grumbling to himself, Lazoen reties his worm and makes what by now must be his 500th cast of the day. But, strangely, he begins to work the worm differently – the way most anglers fish a crankbait. Instead of methodically hopping it through the vegetation, Lazoen begins bringing it back to the boat with a steady retrieve and without using the rod to create action. He is fishing at 45 rpms with a bait that's normally run at 33.

The thought occurs – this guy has spent too much time in the sun. After all, this is Florida, land of the "dead-worming" technique, where the bass have to be finessed with these slinky pieces of plastic to be fooled into biting them. And this guy thinks he is fishing some type of plastic buzzbait.

Suddenly, Lazoen snaps the rod skyward and quickly boats the first bass. It weighs about 4½ pounds. After releasing it, Lazoen makes another cast and his super-fast worm retrieve again gets interrupted – this time by a 2-pounder. In the next 20 casts, Lazoen fills out a five-bass daily limit. Releasing each fish, he remains solemn, concentrating entirely on making long casts across the immense peppergrass bed and this unorthodox retrieve. Finally he speaks, answering some unspoken skepticism that, by now, has waned significantly.

"Most people think I'm crazy, fishing a worm that way," Lazoen says, only to be greeted by my enthusiastic denial. "You've just seen something that has worked for me in tournaments all over the country. From New York to Texas to Nevada, speed-worming has saved many a day for me."

Speed-worming is about as unconventional as plastic worm fishing can get. The rage for many years has been the dead-worming technique, where the worm is regularly paused and then inched across the bottom. In fact, the gospel according to many pros is that the average angler simply fishes a plastic worm too fast.

Then there is Lazoen's method, which has produced well enough on the "Big O" to make him one of the lake's most renowned guides, and consistently enough on the national tournament circuit to make him a successful tournament pro.

Best Conditions for Speed Wormin'

Although the speed-worming technique is most effective in spring and summer, Lazoen has proven it will consistently produce throughout the year in bass waters as diverse as Nevada's Lake Mead, New York's

Larry Lazoen

Larry Lazoen is a B.A.S.S. Tournament winner and eight-time BASS Masters Classic qualifier. A renowned bass and saltwater guide, Lazoen has won more than $400,000 in tournament cash. Lazoen lives in Port Charlotte, Florida.

Hudson River and Texas' Sam Rayburn Reservoir.

It is especially effective on spawning bass in spring. Lazoen has enjoyed remarkable success by throwing the worm well past bedding bass and swimming it through the nest. That usually produces a reaction strike and accounts for 80 percent of the spawners he catches and releases each year.

There are exceptions to the method's year-round allure. As with all techniques, water temperature and bass activity levels are deciding factors. Once the water dips below the 50-degree mark, speed-worming isn't much of an option, Lazoen admits. During those colder-water periods, as well as cold-front conditions when the bass are inactive, Lazoen becomes a "dead-worm" fisherman along with most other avid bass anglers. And speed-worming is not very effective around scattered cover or structure in shallow water on bright, sunny days

when the fish are likely to be holding tight to an object.

Speed-worming works in a wide range of water-clarity conditions. It draws strikes from impressive distances in crystal-clear water, produces consistently in the high visibility of Florida's tannic-colored water, and even scores in muddy water. "Fishing a tournament on [Alabama's] Lake Eufaula, the water we were concentrating on was all roiled up with mud from carp that were spawning," Lazoen recalls. "Yet, speed-worming worked well. I caught a lot more fish than my partners, who were using spinnerbaits."

This unorthodox worming technique is particularly productive in a variety of aquatic vegetation, but can also be effective around isolated woody cover (fallen logs, stumps and treetops) and vertical cover such as boat docks, standing timber and bridge pilings.

This is a particularly effective technique for fishing shallow, weedy flats. "By making long casts across large fields of grass or weeds where bass can be anywhere, your worm is in the strike zone much longer than it would be if you were to use the flipping or pitching technique," Lazoen explains. "The worm is in potential bass-producing water from the time it hits the water until it is in the boat."

Bait Selection

Lazoen utilizes three types of plastic worms for his speed technique.

A classic Culprit ribbon-tail worm is used most often because it has a built-in action when retrieved rapidly. It is particularly effective when buzzed across surface vegetation, but it also works well over sunken weed beds. When fishing a few inches below the surface, Lazoen sometimes uses a slender worm with a sickle-shaped tail. For vegetation that has barely reached the surface, he may switch to a paddle-tail.

The worm weight varies with each situation. A $\frac{1}{8}$-ounce bullet-shaped sinker is well-suited for speed-worming near the sur-

face in light cover or open water, while a $\frac{3}{16}$-ounce weight is better for working through pads or atop matted vegetation. And Lazoen prefers a $\frac{1}{4}$-ounce sinker for fishing the deep hydrilla.

Unlike many anglers, Lazoen never pegs the bullet weight in place with a toothpick or rubber band. "With this technique you're steadily reeling it through the water, so the force of the water keeps the sinker up against the worm," he explains.

If you are starting to get the idea that, as a worm fisherman, Larry Lazoen is a little unconventional, consider that he limits himself to a handful of colors. His absolute favorite is black grape with green glitter.

"That color has worked in every state I've ever fished, including Florida, Texas, New York, Kentucky, Tennessee and out West," Lazoen says. "People tend to make bass fishing too complicated, whether it be worm fishing, spinnerbait fishing or whatever. You don't need to complicate things by running up and down the blade sizes or in and out of the color charts. It is more important to concentrate on

Lazoen's Favorite Worms

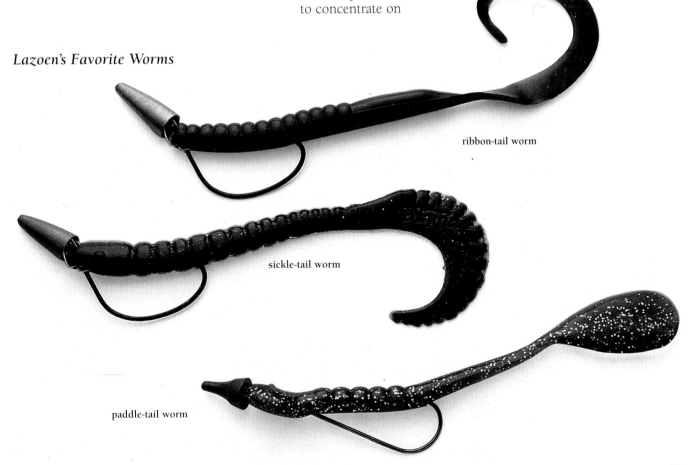

ribbon-tail worm

sickle-tail worm

paddle-tail worm

For fishing scattered or moderately heavy cover, Lazoen uses a 6½-foot graphite rod with a slightly limber tip. For heavy cover, he switches to a rod that has a little more backbone. "A long rod is critical in this type of fishing," Lazoen says. "It allows you to make longer casts and hold your rod high so you can easily regulate the depth of the worm."

Line size is not a major consideration because the bass often hit the worm out of reflex. Lazoen uses 12- to 17-pound clear mono, but recommends that others use the lightest line with which they feel comfortable.

Speed wormin' draws bass out of heavy weeds.

with each technique rather than stocking your tackle box with every color available."

Speed-Wormin' Techniques

Lazoen varies his speed-worming technique somewhat, depending mainly on depth.

Surface fishing – When fishing thick fields of pads as well as heavy, matted vegetation that forms a blanket on the surface, Lazoen works the worm quickly across the top. His retrieve is so fast that it is similar to that used with buzzbait, rubber mouse or frog. The sight of a bass exploding through the jungle of vegetation to inhale the worm is almost heart-stopping.

Subsurface exploring – With scattered vegetation like peppergrass, eelgrass, cabbage and milfoil just below the surface, and boat trails and other cuts through heavier cover, Lazoen uses a steady retrieve

to keep the worm about 2 to 4 inches under the water.

Deep vegetation – Lazoen has had outstanding success with this technique in deep vegetation. On Sam Rayburn Reservoir, for example, where the hydrilla tops out at 6 to 10 feet below the surface, he works the worm much like a swimming plug. He steadily moves it across the top of the weeds, using a high rod position to keep the lure from sinking too deep into the vegetation.

In contrast to his methods for fishing vegetation, Lazoen's approach to working wood is to first move the worm slowly around isolated cover. Then he turns to the speed-worming technique. "You'll be surprised how many times swimming the worm through the same area will trigger a strike," Lazoen claims. "That is especially true if the bass are not holding tight to the cover and are roaming around."

A major attribute of the speed-worming technique is its hook-up ratio. Lazoen believes that the additional speed increases your chances of successfully setting the hook.

"It's not like slow-worm fishing when you'll feel a bump, wonder if it's a fish and maybe not even set the hook," he explains. "Almost all of the bites you get while speed-worming are definite strikes. They'll hit it hard, often several times. And often you'll see the water boil behind the worm. Sometimes you'll see the strike, which allows you to react quickly.

"All you have to do is drop the rod tip to give the fish a little slack, let him swim with it momentarily, reel down until you catch up to him and then set the hook. If you have the presence of mind to do that, you'll catch virtually all of them."

There are times when Lazoen's speed-worming technique must take a back seat to the more conventional style of plastic-worm fishing. But by experimenting with different retrieves on each trip, you'll notice more bass finding their way into your boat.

Speed-Wormin' Over Matted Weeds

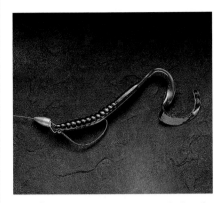

Rig a ⅛-ounce bullet sinker ahead of a ribbon-tail worm. The fish cannot see the bait well but are attracted by the vibration.

Make a long cast over matted vegetation and start reeling before the lure has a chance to sink. Keep your rod tip high and reel fast enough to keep the bait skipping over the weeds.

Speed-Wormin' Just Beneath the Surface

Rig a ³⁄₁₆-ounce bullet sinker ahead of a paddle-tail or sickle-tail worm. The fish are drawn to the flopping, erratic action.

After casting, let the worm sink a few inches and then begin a steady retrieve, just fast enough to keep the worm at the same level as the weed tops.

Speed-Wormin' in Deep Weeds

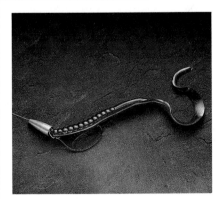

Rig a ¼-ounce bullet sinker ahead of a ribbontail worm. Visibility is limited in the deep water, but bass key on the vibration.

Allow the worm to sink down to the level of the weed tops, then begin reeling slowly, hesitating and dropping the rod tip to allow the worm to sink into deeper pockets.

SPINNERBAITS

A Spinnerbait Primer

by Don Wirth

Charlie Ingram, well-known Tennessee bass pro and TV fishing celebrity, is one of the top-money-winners on the cast-for-cash circuit. Although he's adept at catching bass on every lure style, he'll readily admit to being addicted to spinnerbaits – and for good reason. He's won well over a quarter-million dollars chunking this lure on the pro circuit!

A spinnerbait doesn't look like anything in nature when it's hanging from the pegboard at your local tackle shop. Yet when this lure is in motion, it looks startlingly real. The blades flash like fleeing baitfish. Unlike a wobbling crankbait, the lure has a natural flowing motion, like a fish swimming along.

But you don't have to see a spinnerbait to know it's working. You can feel it right through your rod tip. A spinnerbait pulses and throbs, sending out vibrations that attract bass even in the muddiest, darkest conditions. Bass can feel these vibrations through their lateral line; some experts believe they can even feel them through their eyes. No wonder a spinnerbait is the deadliest of all bass lures in low-visibility conditions.

Despite the proven effectiveness of spinnerbaits, some bass anglers have little regard for them, contending that they're "no-brainer" lures. If you're in that category, be prepared for a rude awakening.

Here, the Tennessee pro shares his spinnerbait secrets with NAFC members. Heed his advice – it will definitely make you a better bass angler.

Selecting a Spinnerbait

At first glance, most spinnerbaits look pretty much alike, but closer inspection will reveal subtle, yet important, differences.

The key components of any spinnerbait are its weighted head, wire frame, blade(s), hook and skirt.

The metal head gives the lure casting weight. Spinnerbaits are rated according to their head weight – 1/4 ounce, 3/8 ounce, 1 ounce, etc. Heavy heads are ideal for working deep dropoffs and ledges. Lighter heads are used for running the lure in shallow water and over the tops of submerged mossbeds. The lure's head is designed to bump off and slide over underwater objects. Ingram uses a 3/8- to 9/10- ounce spinnerbait most of the time in what he calls "classic spinnerbait water" – murky and fairly shallow. Heavier lures are great in shallow, clear water when the wind comes up and you need to make an extra-long cast to avoid spooking the fish.

The wire arm provides the framework for the lure. If you fish a variety of spinnerbaits, you'll notice that some of them put out more vibration than others. The lighter the wire, the more vibration a spinnerbait will produce. But you can't use wire that's too light or a big bass will tear the lure to pieces.

Charlie Ingram

Charlie Ingram, host of cable TV's "Fishing University," is one of the all-time leading money winners on the pro-bass circuit. He has the distinction of being the only professional angler to win three B.A.S.S. events in one year.

A shallow-water specialist, Ingram considers the spinnerbait his number-one lure and has used it in many of his tournament victories.

Ingram resides in Columbia, Tennessee.

Parts of a Spinnerbait

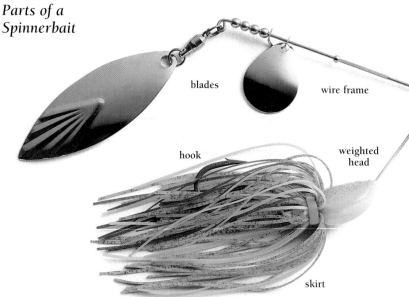

blades

wire frame

hook

weighted head

skirt

Ingram now uses spinnerbaits made with a titanium wire frame. This is incredibly light, yet very strong. "It produces vibrations that'll just about knock your fillings loose when you retrieve the lure," Ingram says.

You often hear bass fishermen refer to "long-arm" or "short-arm" spinnerbaits. The length of the arm is a critical factor determining how much vibration the bait will put out when in motion. The shorter the arm to which the blades are attached, the more vibration is typically produced. Short-arm spinnerbaits are great in low-visibility conditions – in muddy water, and at night. A long-arm spinnerbait, on the other hand, is a better choice when fishing in heavy cover. While the longer arm causes the lure to emit less intense vibrations, this design helps it slide through, around and over submerged objects more easily.

The hooks of most spinnerbaits on the market today are strong and sharp, but Ingram routinely touches them up with a diamond file. This may make the difference between one or two extra fish in the boat in a day's fishing, and that translates into money in the bank.

Here's an inside tip: Always make sure the hook point is aimed directly at the place where your line ties to the lure! This is the straightest line to deep hook penetration.

Colorado (top), willow-leaf (middle) and Indiana (bottom) blades.

Often the hook point will get bumped out of kilter slightly when you catch a bass, or when working the lure through stumps or rocks. Bend the point as directed and you'll get more hookups, usually without having to rear back and set the hook hard.

The spinnerbait skirt is usually made of rubber or a soft synthetic material like silicone. Ingram prefers silicone over real rubber in clear water – it comes in translucent or clear colors that make it look more lifelike. But a rubber skirt produces more vibrations, so it works better in murky water.

Most factory-assembled spinnerbaits have the skirt on "backwards," so it puffs out. This helps give the lure a lifelike "breathing" action. The skirt is the primary color component of most spinnerbaits, so keep several spare skirts in different colors in your tackle box and change them according to conditions.

Good skirt colors include clear and smoke (clear water), white and green (stained water), black and purple (muddy water, or at night).

The blades are another critical element of any spinnerbait. Most spinnerbaits have one or two blades; the latter are referred to as "tandems."

Blades come in three different designs: willow-leaf (long and slender), Colorado (short and rounded) and Indiana (teardrop-shaped – neither as rounded as a Colorado, nor as elongated as a willow-leaf). Various hybrids of the three are available, but these are the main styles you should be familiar with.

One of the key decisions you'll make when fishing a spinnerbait is choosing which blade style to use. There are days when it really doesn't matter which type you throw at the bass – they seem to bite anything. But most of the time, bass aren't quite that active, so using the right blade style can make a real difference in the quantity and quality of bass you'll catch.

The willow-leaf blade resembles a slender baitfish as it flashes through the water. In clear water on a sunny day, a tandem willow-leaf puts out so much flash, it actually appears to be an entire school of baitfish. Flash is good, but there's a tradeoff. Compared to the Colorado and Indiana styles, a willow-leaf blade puts out less vibration.

long arm

short arm

Spinnerbait Trailers

Ingram often fishes a trailer on his spinnerbait. Good trailers include pork or plastic frogs, plastic grubs and split-tail eels.

Use a trailer when you want to give the lure more bulk. This makes it more visible in murky water and can present a more appealing profile to a big, hungry bass. Trailers are also useful when you want to "float" the lure above submerged weedbeds, or to make it sink slower when fishing deep ledges.

Trailers help fine-tune your color presentation. In murky water, put a hot pink or chartreuse trailer on a white spinnerbait. In general, the clearer the water, the more unobtrusive your trailer should be. When bass are spooky or slow to bite after a cold front, the lure generally produces better without a trailer.

Frogs

Grubs

Split-tail eel

Changing blades takes only a few seconds.

Ingram uses a willow-leaf spinnerbait for most clear-water applications, and for fishing around grassbeds– the slender blade seems to slide through sparse grass more easily than other blade styles. He also favors it whenever bass are spooky and reluctant to bite.

When the water is murky or muddy, and at night under any water clarity condition, Ingram leans toward a Colorado blade. This style has less flash than a willow-leaf, but considerably more vibration. It is heavily cupped to create a distinct throbbing action. Use it whenever bass are having a hard time seeing your lure. The intense vibration it puts out will help them find it even under the lowest-visibility conditions.

The Indiana blade style works great in stained water. It has more visual appeal than a Colorado but not quite as much "throb." It's a good compromise blade under most shallow bassin' situations.

Blade color is another factor to consider. Unpainted blades are the most popular, but painted blades have made a big impact on the bass fishing scene lately. Ingram usually fishes painted blades when visibility is low. Blades used for bass range from size 1 (the smallest) to size 7 (the largest).

You can order spinnerbait blades from a tackle outlet and keep them in your tackle box. With a pair of split-ring pliers, it's easy

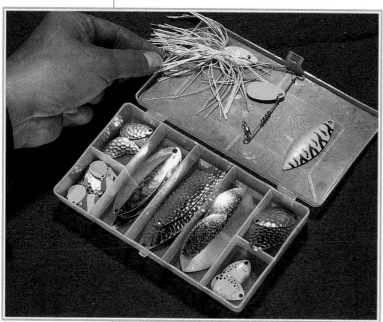

Recommended Tackle

A 6- to 6½-foot medium-action baitcasting outfit is ideal for most spinnerbait fishing. Avoid a stiff rod – you'll pull the bait away from the fish when it strikes. A 7-foot rod is a better choice in clear or deep water. It allows extra-long casts and gives you a lot of control over a fish in deep cover.

A slow-retrieve baitcasting reel has plenty of winching power to help you bull-dog a big bass out of heavy brush or stumps. Spool up with abrasion-resistant mono or super-line, from 14- to 20-pound test.

to change blade styles, sizes and finishes quickly as conditions change; this is a lot cheaper than buying a big assortment of complete lures with different blade shapes and sizes.

Spinnerbait Techniques

Most anglers just cast out a spinnerbait and reel it in, without giving much thought to varying the retrieve depth, speed or consistency. And amazingly enough, the cast-and-reel routine will catch a lot of bass under most conditions.

But fine-tuning your approach can make these baits even more effective. Here are some techniques you can use to greatly enhance your catch with this lure.

Many bass fishermen are not sure how deep or how fast they should be fishing their spinnerbait. This will vary from one lake to the next, even from one part of a lake to another. But there's really no mystery to determining the right depth or retrieve speed no matter where you're fishing. Here's how to do it right every time.

When fishing a spinnerbait in water no deeper than 10 feet, place a visual emphasis on the retrieve. Stand up, wear polarized sunglasses and keep your eyes on the lure. Over years of intense practice with a spinnerbait, Ingram has found that he catches more fish on it when he fishes it at a level where he can barely see the blades flashing. He refers to this level as the "twilight zone".

Water clarity and light conditions will help determine where the twilight zone is on any given day. Let's say you're fishing a stained creek arm on a cloudy morning. You'll have to keep the spinnerbait pretty close to the surface to see any blade flash. But later in the morning, when the clouds dissipate and light penetration is more intense, you can see the blades flash much more easily. That's when you should slow down the retrieve so the lure drops deeper. In muddy water, try fishing the lure so fast and close to the top, the blades actually break the surface.

This simple visual adjustment technique bypasses much of the guesswork involved in spinnerbait fishing. You don't have to worry about how deep or how fast you should retrieve the lure no matter where you're fishing it – just keep it where you can barely see it with the naked eye.

A spinnerbait isn't totally weedless, but it is ideal for fishing around shallow solid objects like rocks, submerged logs, stumps, etc. You will find that many strikes occur immediately after your lure makes contact with an underwater object. This is because the bait changes speed and direction slightly when bumping into a stump or rock, making it appear much more lifelike. When a baitfish panics, it doesn't keep swimming in a straight line, but rather veers quickly to one side or another. Banging the lure into submerged objects simulates this flight behavior.

Always try to maximize the amount of contact your spinnerbait has with a particular object. The classic example is a sub-merged tree in shallow water. You could cast the lure crossways to the tree; it will swim through open water, bump the tree once, then swim through more open water. A better approach would be to cast the spinnerbait so it runs down the entire length of the tree, bumping it in several spots during the retrieve.

When working a spinnerbait, use the lure to comb the "edges" connecting two different types of structure or cover. Bass often congregate in these spots. For example, one likely edge for spinnerbaiting is the weedline created where a patch of submerged grass meets open water. Another is the outer perimeter of a stump row. When fishing edges, cast the lure parallel to the spot where one type of cover meets another, or where cover meets open water. This will maximize the time the bait spends in the "edge" zone, which is generally the most productive area.

Take Charlie Ingram's advice and sharpen your spinnerbait skills. "Day in and day out, a spinnerbait will be the most versatile and dependable lure in your tackle box," he promises.

Working the Edges

Work a weedline by casting parallel to the edge where the weeds meet open water. Bass tend to relate to this edge, so the casting angle is of utmost importance.

When casting to stumps or standing timber, line up your cast so the lure passes near or bumps as many stumps or trees as possible.

How to "Tune" a Spinnerbait

Bend the upper arm of your spinnerbait so it aligns with the hook. If the arm is bent to the side, the bait will run at a tilt.

Check your hook point to make sure it is is aimed directly at the spinnerbait's attachment eye. This ensures maximum hook penetration.

Four Spinnerbaiting Tips

To make a spinnerbait run deeper, pinch a Rubber-cor sinker (without the rubber) onto the hook shank.

Add a stinger hook to catch short strikers. Slip a short piece of rubber tubing over the eye of the stinger, then push the spinnerbait hook through the eye.

Attach a stinger hook point up for heavy cover (left); point down for light cover (right). The latter method maximizes your hooking percentage.

Don't use spinnerbaits with a thin-wire shaft and a hairpin-style attachment eye. Constant bending may fatigue the wire and cause it to break.

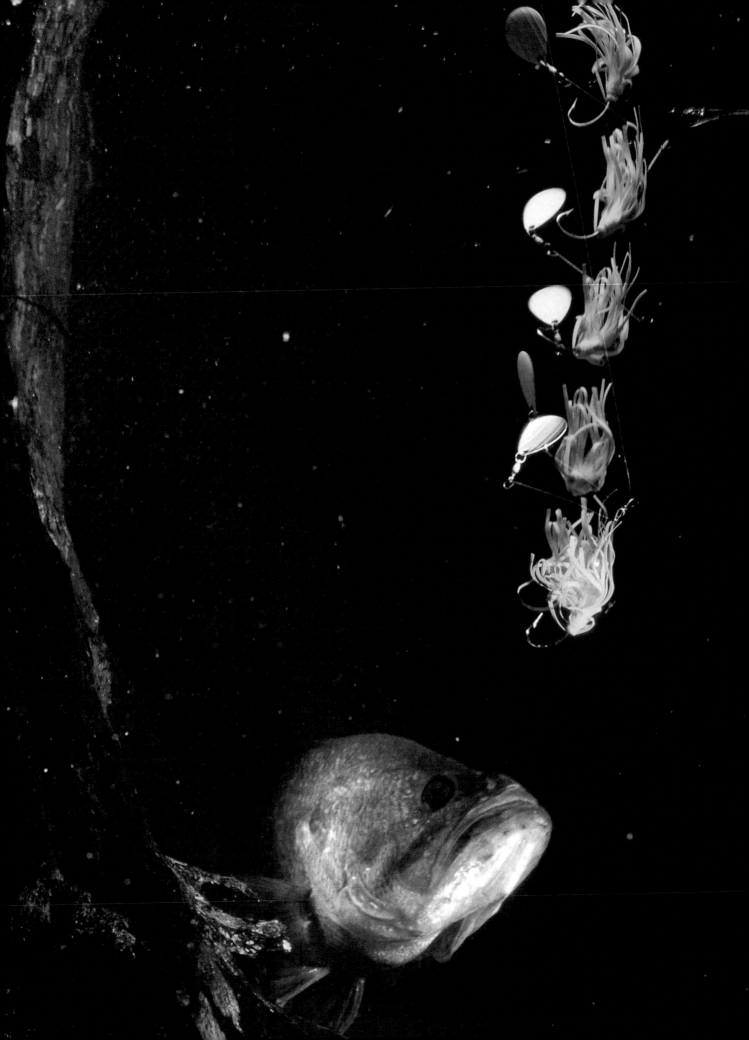

Big Blades
for Deepwater Bass

By Ronnie Kovach

Beginning bass anglers often make the mistake of assuming that spinnerbaits are primarily a warm-weather, shallow-water option. The fact of the matter is that many tournament anglers and professional guides rely extensively on spinnerbaits, particularly jumbo versions of these baits, for catching bass in late fall and winter, when the fish move into deep water.

During coldwater periods, all the major bass species – largemouths, smallmouths and spots – are in somewhat of a metabolic slowdown. Yet they will continue to feed and strike lures until the water temperature dips below the 45°F mark. There will be occasional sunny days when the bass move up into shallow water and feed aggressively near the bank. But, more often, they'll be at depths of at least 15 feet and they may go as deep as 60.

If you know where the bass are hanging out in coldwater periods, you can thoroughly work these spots with a "slow" bait, such as a jig or jigging spoon. But when you're unsure of their location, you need a faster bait that will cover more water.

Largemouths commonly form tight schools during the coldwater months. Once these schools are established, the fish are not likely to move far until the water begins to warm up. Some savvy anglers use big spinnerbaits to search out these concentrations, and then switch to slower baits to work these spots more thoroughly.

The $1/8$- to $1/2$-ounce spinnerbaits that most anglers throw during the summer months are effective only down to a depth of about 15 feet. For locating and catching deepwater bass, most top tournament pros and guides rely on spinnerbaits weighing 1 to $1/2$ ounces. These baits can be bounced along the bottom and allowed to "helicopter" into deepwater bass haunts, creating an action that can't be achieved with any other type of lure.

Before you start cramming your tackle box with big blades, however, you need to understand the the specific lure designs that work best under different conditions, the most effective retrieves and the recommended tackle.

Prime Locations for
Deepwater Spinnerbaiting

Deep brushy bottoms often hold bass in cold-water periods. Slow-roll the spinnerbait so it just brushes the top of the woody cover.

Bass often hold along steep, rocky ledges. Cast a spinnerbait to the lip of the ledge and let it helicopter down the break.

Selecting Deepwater Spinnerbaits

A good deepwater spinnerbait must meet three primary criteria:

• It must be heavy enough to sink quickly into the depths the bass are using.

• The blades must be able to turn at a very slow retrieve speed, because it takes a slow-moving bait to draw strikes in cold water.

• The bait must present a large profile, not so much because bass tend to feed on larger forage items in coldwater periods, but the larger profile helps get their attention and draw reaction strikes.

You may be able to get by with a ¾-ounce spinnerbait when the fish are holding around the 20-foot mark, but when they're at 40 feet or more, a 1½-ounce model would be much more effective.

The trend in shallow-water spinnerbaits has been toward willow-leaf blades, because their long, thin shape makes them more weed-resistant than other blade styles. But willow-leafs require more speed to get them turning than do other blade types. This explains why most deepwater spinnerbaits come with the wider Colorado blades or a combination of Colorado and Indiana blades.

In summer, the majority of bass anglers throw spinnerbaits with size 4 or 5 blades. But when the fish go deep in coldwater periods, most fishermen switch to size 6 or 7 blades and some even go to size 8.

Spinnerbait manufacturer and avid bass fisherman Bob Suekawa of Haddock Lures, says that these cold-weather requirements are reflected in his spinnerbait orders. "As it gets colder," observes Suekawa, "I see an increase in sales of spinnerbaits with larger Colorado blades instead of jumbo willow-leafs. Here in the West, it started up north at lakes like Shasta, Clear, and Oroville. Now it is common to see western pros throwing 1- to 1½- ounce spinnerbaits with size 6 to 8 Colorado blades or Indiana/Colorado tandem combinations in the coldest water."

Some coldwater spinnerbaiters have found that the rather obscure "twin-spin" is an excellent option. The twin-spin differs from the classic single-spin in that it has two upper arms instead of one. Twin-spins are particularly deadly during coldwater periods because they helicopter so slowly. They also have a slightly different sound and action than a single spin; the smaller Colorado or Indiana blades produce a more modest flash and a softer whirring sensation, which some experts believe is more attractive to semi-lethargic, suspended bass.

Another option to achieve better helicoptering is to use a spinnerbait with a shorter-than-usual upper arm. Some manufacturers offer short-arm

Blade-Size Chart

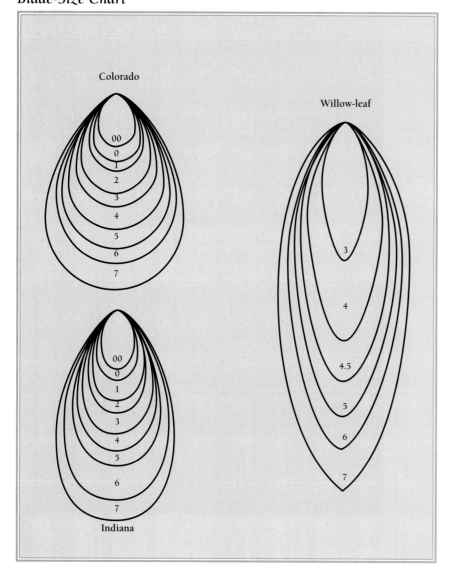

How to Modify a Spinnerbait for Helicoptering

1 *Cut off about an inch of the upper arm of your spinnerbait to make it helicopter better.*

2 *Reattach the swivel and blade by bending a new loop in the shaft, as shown.*

Popular Deepwater Spinnerbaits

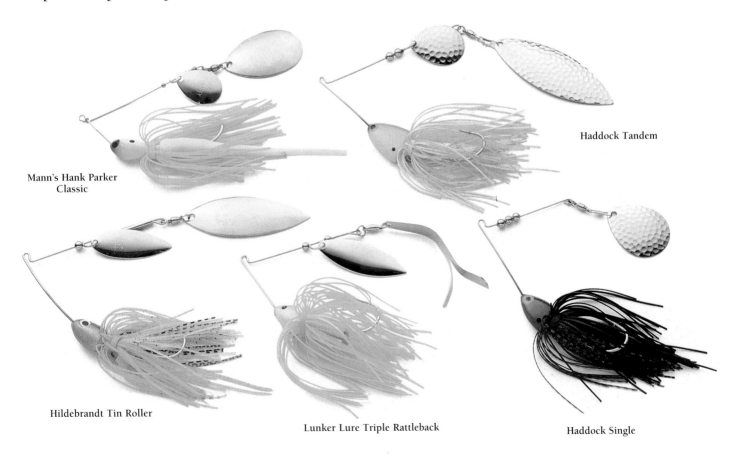

Mann's Hank Parker
Classic

Haddock Tandem

Hildebrandt Tin Roller

Lunker Lure Triple Rattleback

Haddock Single

Most deep-water spinnerbaiters prefer a 6½- to 7½-foot, medium-heavy-power, fast-action baitcasting rod and a medium-speed reel spooled with 14-pound mono.

The long, fairly stiff rod helps get firm hook sets in the deep water. If line stretch is a problem, try spooling up with 20-pound superline.

Spinnerbaiting in cover.

models, but if you can't find them, you can easily make your own by shortening the arm as shown on page 107. Short-arm models are designed specifically for helicoptering and usually have a single size 6 to 8 Colorado blade.

Spinnerbaiting in Deep Water

The key to fishing spinnerbaits in deep, cold water is learning to really S-L-O-W down! Even though these lures are reaction baits, it may be difficult to get bass to "react" in water this cold. The fish are lethargic and aren't likely to swim very far or very fast to bushwhack a lure. The best advice is to retrieve the spinnerbait just fast enough for the blades to keep spinning.

There are two main methods for fishing big spinnerbaits in deep water: slow-rolling them along the bottom or helicoptering them alongside deep cover or structure.

Slow-rolling means retrieving just fast enough to make the blades spin. In most cases, the bait is allowed to bump the bottom or make contact with brush, weedtops or other cover as it moves along. The erratic action caused by the blades ticking the cover seems to trigger strikes.

Helicoptering means allowing the bait to sink vertically with the spinning blade slowing its descent. The larger the blade and the more easily it spins, the slower the bait will fall. If the bait sinks rapidly, coldwater bass will usually ignore it. Helicoptering is the ideal presentation when bass are tucked in tight to vertical cover, such as standing timber or a steep cliff face.

It's not unusual for a bass to grab a spinnerbait "on the fall" during warmwater periods, but the likelihood of this type of take is even stronger in cold water. It's common for coldwater bass to ignore a spinnerbait retrieved horizontally, but immediately grab it the second it begins to helicopter.

A strike can come anytime during the fall, so it's important to keep your line semi-taut, but not tight, until the bait sinks all the way to the bottom. If you allow the line to go slack, you won't be able to detect the subtle "tick" that signals a take. With this type of vertical presentation, it's not unusual for bass to grab the bait at depths of 50 feet or more.

When the bait is helicoptering properly, you'll feel the blade thumping; if you don't feel the vibration, the blade may be hung up. But if the blade is spinning properly and suddenly stops, a bass may have grabbed the bait; set the hook.

When casting to deep, vertical cover, it's important to feed line as the bait helicopters. If you engage your reel too soon, the bait will swing away from the cover and toward your boat. There is a delicate balance between keeping the line tight enough to detect a take and preventing it from swinging away from the target.

It takes a sensitive rod to feel the thumping of the blade, especially when the line is not tight. That explains why most anglers opt for a high-modulus, fast-action graphite rod. But a strong case can be made for fishing big blades with a softer fiberglass rod.

Recently, while doing some deep spinnerbaiting with western pro Dave Mitchell, I watched him outfish me 15 to 2 on solid 2- to 3-pound winter largemouths. I was using a standard graphite baitcaster; he had a whippier, soft fiberglass model.

After thoroughly showing me up, Mitchell demonstrated how the soft-tip rod allowed him to better feel the strike with the big spinnerbaits. The fiberglass rod also flexed enough so that he was able to use a much softer hook set on fish that were barely mouthing the lure.

"The problem," Mitchell explained, "is that your stiffer graphite rod may not detect these softer spinnerbait strikes in the winter. When it does, it forces you to pull the big baits out of the fish's mouth."

Practically everything we read about spinnerbaits depicts them as shallow-water, dense-cover lures. If you're one of the millions of bass anglers that look at them this way, it may be time to readjust your thinking.

Three Tips for Deepwater Spinnerbaiting

Add a good-size pork trailer to slow the bait's descent and draw more strikes. A pork trailer works better than a plastic one because it is more buoyant.

Use a spinnerbait with the "Speed Blade" design, which allows you to easily change blades. This way, you can switch blade sizes and colors to suit the conditions.

Feed line while your spinnerbait helicopters down a submerged tree or other vertical cover (red line). If your line is too tight, the bait will swing away (black line).

Spinnerbait Secrets

Roland Martin Reveals his Deadly Spinnerbaiting System

By Tim Tucker

Roland Martin is a system-oriented angler. Every part of his fishing attack has a program, a game plan.

And he attributes his systematic approach to individual lures as a major reason why he is the most successful tournament fisherman of all time, with 19 B.A.S.S. tournament victories and nine Angler of the Year awards to his credit.

"I developed systems for each type of bait, so that I would have the right weapon for almost any condition – particularly water clarity, which is extremely important, but often overlooked by the average fisherman," Martin says. "If you aren't using the right type of lure in the right water clarity, you're wasting your time. "That's particularly true with spinnerbaits."

Several years ago, Martin eliminated guess work for the average fisherman by developing the Roland Martin Spinnerbait Series for Blue Fox.

"There are really three types of water," Martin explains. "So I designed a system for Blue Fox for fishing each type of water – clear, dark and muddy. By changing skirt color and the color and size of the blade, I came up with the most effective baits for those different situations based on all of the years of experience I have fishing all around the country.

"These spinnerbaits, colors, size and blades came from the system of spinnerbait fishing that I used for years on my own."

Fishing Spinnerbaits in Clear Water

"There are a tremendous number of problems involved with fishing spinnerbaits in clear water," Martin contends. "On a bright, sunny day in clear water, you're just wasting your time.

"With clear water, you have fewer opportunities to catch bass on a spinnerbait. Spinnerbaits aren't made for clear-water fishing. You're going to have a hard time catching fish unless you have certain conditions."

"Since clear water increases the fish's opportunity to examine the spinnerbait more closely and also see you from a greater distance, it's important to fish in low-light conditions," Martin advises. "A windy, rainy day is the best time to fish a clear-water lake like Table Rock (in Missouri) or Lake Mead (near Las Vegas) in the summertime."

"In clear water, your best chances of catching bass are early in the morning and late in the evening," he adds. "And with the right amount of wind, you can catch fish all day, even on a real clear lake. A 25-mile-an-hour wind blowing big waves into the

Roland Martin

Roland Martin is one of sport fishing's living legends. A member of the international Fishing Hall of Fame, Martin owns B.A.S.S. records for most tournament victories and "Angler of the Year" titles.

A 21-time BASS Masters Classic qualifier, he is host of "Fishing with Roland Martin," one of the longest-running fishing shows on television. Martin hails from Clewiston, Florida.

shoreline creates turbidity and a lot of light refraction. When there are no waves, the light penetrates deep because the surface is flat. The rougher the surface, the less light penetration there is.

"I've learned from diving and filming in clear lakes that the rougher the water, the darker the water is when you get down deep. That enables you to get away with throwing a spinnerbait in clear water. The

fish can't see it or you nearly as well. If it's a bright, clear, calm sunny day on Table Rock, you just don't throw a spinnerbait."

But Martin points out that a spinnerbait can be deadly at night on a clear lake.

"In clear water, I like a spinnerbait with a willow-leaf blade", Martin says. "White is the most productive clear-water skirt color, and black is extremely effective for fishing at night.

A spinnerbait with a white skirt is the best choice in clear water.

Martin's Favorite Clear-Water Spinnerbaits

Ultraclear Water -
#2 nickel blade,
white skirt

Night Fishing - #5 black blade,
black skirt

Clear Water -
#5 nickel blade,
white skirt

Recommended Tackle

Martin uses two different types of outfits for his spinnerbait fishing, depending on whether he's target fishing or working large weed flats.

Target Fishing — You'll need a 5½-foot medium-power baitcaster with a limber tip for good casting accuracy. Combine this with a medium-speed baitcasting reel.

Weed-Flat Fishing — Use a 7-foot medium-power baitcaster with a long handle for making two-handed power casts. The distance is necessary to cover expansive weed flats. Use the same type of reel as you would for target fishing.

Your choice of line depends on water clarity. For clear water, Martin uses 8- to 10-pound-test mono; for dark or muddy water, 30-pound superline or 17- to 25-pound mono.

"In real clear water, I'll normally drop down to a smaller blade, like a size 2 nickel. But I once used a bait with a size 5 nickel-colored willow-leaf blade and a white skirt to place high in the money in a tournament on Truman Reservoir. I was buzzing the tops of trees in clear water about 35 feet deep, but the fish were suspended in the treetops. In practice, I caught five fish that weighed 25 pounds on that bait."

Spinnerbaiting in clear water requires lighter line and longer casts. But Martin breaks away from the traditional line of thinking about light-line fishing. Instead of using ultralight tackle to cast the light line, Martin has learned to handle the smaller line sizes with heavy gear.

Chartreuse blades show up in dark or muddy water.

Dark Water – In dark water, Martin uses a blade combination of gold and copper. He often teams a size 4 or 5 gold blade with a size 1 copper.

The two most productive skirt colors in dark water are chartreuse and white. Other productive colors include yellow-and-green or yellow-and-blue.

"It's dark water, so you need to make noise with the spinnerbait," Martin says. "But the fish have some visibility. They can see from farther away. You don't need quite as big a blade or quite as bright a color as you would with muddy water, yet you need a little more than in real clear water."

Muddy Water – "In muddy water, you're interested in making a lot of noise and having a bright lure," Martin says. "To fish a spinnerbait effectively in muddy water, you need hot muddy water. You don't want cold muddy water. The only time fish will bite in real muddy water is during hot weather. So that means fishing muddy water in the summertime."

For muddy water conditions, Martin uses the most visible skirts and blades available. The skirt color is usually chartreuse or chartreuse-and-blue, and he moves up to a size 3 or 4 Colorado blade, usually copper-colored. If the water is extremely muddy, he uses a fluorescent orange blade.

Larger blades, like a size 5 willow-leaf, make even more noise. Since muddy water allows very little visibility, the noise and vibration of the larger blade often prove to be the strike stimuli.

"With spinnerbait fishing in all types of water, the most important thing to remember is you need to bump the stump," Martin says. "That's particularly true with muddy water.

"That technique of hitting the cover is so important. If a bass is in a foot of water and it's muddy and he's in behind a log, he has a very limited field of vision. He can't see very far in front of him. That log gives him cover, concealment and protection. It also gives him some shade and an ambush point. So you need to break his little sphere of contentment.

"I want the big rod, so I can really set the hook," he says. "That light line is going to stretch and the little rods will only give you about 2 pounds of pressure. You lose a lot of fish because of that."

Fishing Spinnerbaits in Dark or Muddy Water

What Martin calls "dark" water has considerably greater clarity than "muddy" water. "Dark water includes off-colored waters like the St. Johns River in Florida, where there's a lot of tannic acid, as well as many tannic-stained reservoirs in New England and the marshy areas of Wisconsin and Minnesota," Martin explains. "You'll also find dark, stained water on the coastal

"You need to come blowing right through that sphere with a big-bladed spinnerbait. That intimidates, alerts and scares him at the same time. The pugnacious nature of a bass is such that he will normally hold his ground and hit that lure. But there's a limit to what those fish will take. In other words, the sound, the noise and the color of a spinnerbait all have a place, but you can over-do it. You can scare a fish with too noisy of a lure and too close of a presentation.

"A lot of it is in the basic cast, the basic presentation of the spinnerbait. I'm using a big lure and it's noisy. When it hits the water, it's going to scare every fish within 5 feet of it. So you don't want to throw it that close to the cover you're fishing. You want to throw it 10 or 15 feet beyond where you think that bass might be holding. A 10-pound bass is a big old, nasty fish, but a half-ounce spinnerbait with a size 7 willow-leaf blade landing 2 feet from him will send him running.

Use a large willow-leaf spinnerbait in extremely muddy water.

Martin's Favorite Dark-Water Spinnerbaits

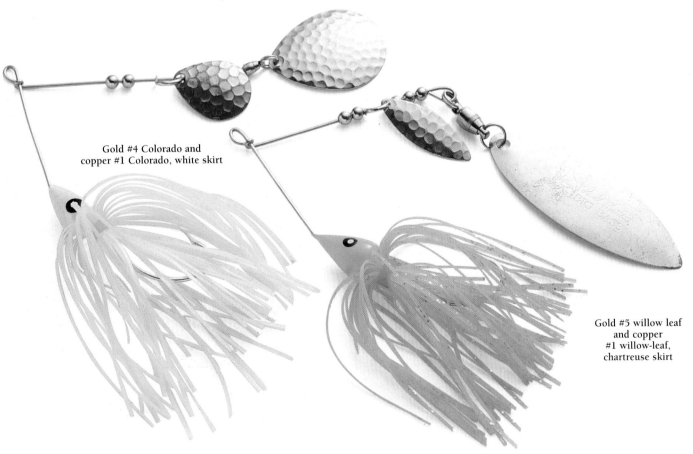

Gold #4 Colorado and
copper #1 Colorado, white skirt

Gold #5 willow leaf
and copper
#1 willow-leaf,
chartreuse skirt

"The proper presentation is to cast it 10 feet past the fish. He'll hear it hit the water that far away, but it's not close enough to scare him. It slightly intimidates him. He hears it coming. He hears that loud vibration and you want it to come right at him on a direct collision course. Then, he'll probably hit it."

Since Martin's most effective spinnerbait technique involves running the lure into the underwater stumps or boat dock pilings he believes holds a bass, he is often unable to use a trailer hook. "But I'll use one any time I can get away with it," he adds. "If I can bump that spinnerbait over a few stumps and keep the trailer on without getting hung up a lot, that's fine.

"Getting hung up a lot is a problem, but it's important to remember that trailer hooks will catch you more fish. If you used a trailer hook all of the time, you'd definitely catch more fish on it."

Martin also prefers to use a plastic trailer for most of his spinnerbait fishing – a Burke Twin Tail or 3- or 4-inch Mister Twister Phenom worm in either white, chartreuse or black.

Although large spinnerbaits have become popular in recent years, the bulk of Martin's spinnerbait fishing involves small baits.

"I work a lot with smaller spinnerbaits," he says. "I rely on the quarter-ounce size for most of my spinnerbait fishing. I can cast the smaller spinnerbait real well and it seems more weedless. I can go through more places with it.

"And that's important because a spinnerbait is not an open-water bait. That's not where it's most effective. I run my spinnerbaits through the thickest, most impenetrable cover I can find. I run it through the heaviest grass or the biggest logjam. Those are places where bass, particularly big bass, are found. You can't be afraid of losing a spinnerbait in heavy cover if you want to be successful."

Roland Martin learned a long time ago that the systematic approach to spinnerbait fishing, dictated by water clarity, is the most effective way to consistently catch fish. And with his track record, who would hesitate to take his advice?

Martin's Favorite Muddy Water Spinnerbaits

#3 copper Colorado blade, chartreuse and blue skirt

#5 flourescent orange willow-leaf blade, chartreuse skirt

Shallow flats with lots of logs and stumps make ideal hangouts for muddy water bass. With the low water clarity, the lack of depth is not a problem. However, the most productive flats are adjacent to deep water

Boat docks may offer the best hiding spots in waters that have little natural cover. Again, the best docks have deep water just off the end.

Back ends of creek arms usually have an abundance of brushy cover. The most productive creek arms are fed by an active creek.

Timbered points with an extended lip are excellent bass producers. The fish feed atop the shallow lip and rest in deep water off to the side.

Weedlines that form along irregular structure have plenty of points and inside turns that attract largemouth bass.

TOPWATERS

Buzzin' for Lunker Bass

by Don Wirth

If you want to experience the full predatorial power of a bass, tease it into blasting a buzzbait. This lure triggers incredible strikes from lunker largemouths – smallmouths, too!

Most anglers think of a buzzbait as the classic "reaction lure." They believe when it churns and sputters noisily across the surface, bass strike it not because they're hungry, but out of sheer orneriness.

I question whether slapping at anything that moves noisily overhead is productive behavior for a bass. This sort of wanton aggressiveness could get a fish into trouble in a hurry. Nature rewards cautious behavior.

I actually believe largemouths find a buzzbait to be quite realistic. When in motion, it resembles a baitfish or small bluegill fleeing from a predator, or a frog skipping across the surface. Don't forget, a buzzbait is a big-bass lure – and bass don't reach lunker size by hitting something they don't perceive as real food.

A buzzbait can be worked through all but the densest cover. The single hook rides upright, allowing you to work the bait across partially submerged logs and stickups where big bass lurk.

Tarpon Springs, Florida, bass guide Captain Ray Van Horn is a master with the buzzbait. He's caught largemouths over 13 pounds on this noisy lure, and knows when, where and how to fish it.

Selecting the Right Buzzbait

When making your buzzbait selection, consider the following:

Lure size – This depends mainly on wind conditions and water clarity. On flat-calm days where the water is fairly clear, a small buzzbait is ideal. Visibility is good under these conditions, calling for a more subtle approach. A big, noisily churning buzzer may spook the bass, but a small one that sputters with a more unobtrusive sound will usually get plastered.

On windy days, use a bigger buzzbait, which will be more visible when there's a chop on the water. But a big buzzer is extremely wind-resistant and difficult to cast, so you'll have to adjust your antibacklash device to prevent overruns.

Color – Color is of minimal importance when using a buzzbait. If you stick with basic colors like white and black, you'll catch bass. In lakes with lots of sunfish, try a buzzer with an orange-and-chartreuse skirt.

Trailer hooks – A buzzbait can be fished with a trailer hook. This will increase your percentage of hookups when bass are striking behind the lure, which they often do when not overly aggressive. But a trailer hook is not advised when working the lure over partially-submerged wood or stringy weeds, because it often tangles in the cover.

Captain Ray Van Horn

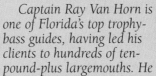

Captain Ray Van Horn is one of Florida's top trophy-bass guides, having led his clients to hundreds of ten-pound-plus largemouths. He also offers saltwater charters for snook and tarpon.

Van Horn is a true fishing innovator, never content with the usual lure or live-bait approaches. His success with buzzbaits, for instance, flies in the face of the usual wisdom that trophy bass seldom strike topwaters.

Van Horn resides in Tarpon Springs, Florida.

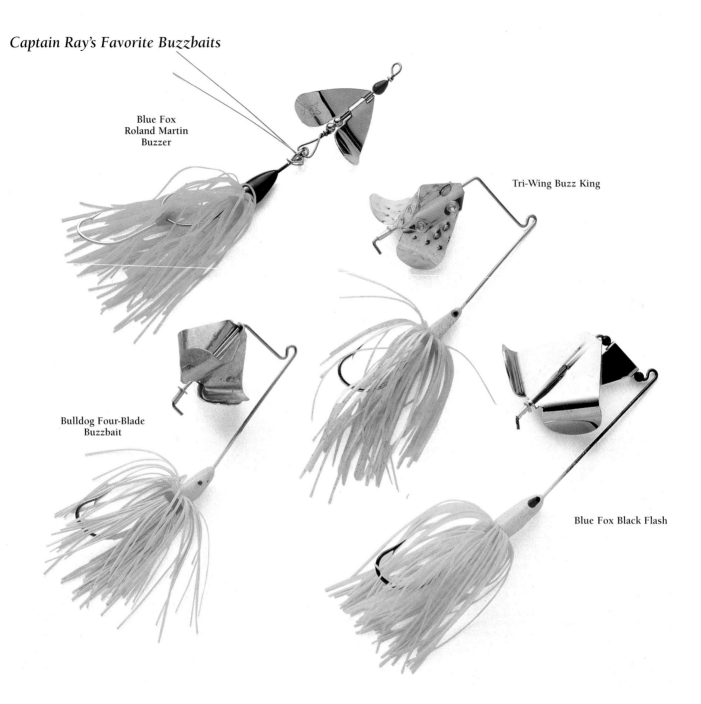

Captain Ray's Favorite Buzzbaits

Blue Fox
Roland Martin
Buzzer

Tri-Wing Buzz King

Bulldog Four-Blade
Buzzbait

Blue Fox Black Flash

When & Where to Fish Buzzbaits

Buzzbaits don't work everywhere. Here are the best conditions in which to fish them, according to Captain Ray:

In warm water – Ideal buzzbait water is somewhere between 65 and 90°F. You seldom have much luck on buzzers in water below 50°F.

Over and around shallow cover – Look for stumps, submerged trees or weed beds that top out just beneath the surface in shallow coves, flats and creek arms. This is clas-

sic buzzbait water. The lure's design allows it to be fished right over most types of cover (except heavy grass, surface scum or lily pads) without hanging up. Always target isolated pieces of cover for the biggest bass.

Around boat docks – A buzzbait is great around boat docks. The best docks extend a long way out over the water and have a grassy shoreline under them and to either side. Dock areas that have been sprayed for weed control are less productive.

Over rocks and boulders –- Most fishermen don't think of a buzzbait when fishing this type of cover, but in clear lakes, it can

In-Line vs. Safety-Pin Buzzers

by Tim Tucker

There are two basic types of buzzbaits that have evolved through decades of bass fishing. Knowledgeable bass fishermen utilize both in different situations. And therein lies the key to buzzbaits becoming a more productive tool more of the time.

The in-line buzzbait has the blade and hook on the same shaft and usually features a bucktail skirt. The second standard type of buzzbait is the safety-pin design (often called an offset buzzbait) that sports a live-rubber skirt, a hook on one arm and a rotating blade on the other.

Both of the basic buzzbait types are distinctly different and serve different purposes. An in-line lure, says former

Classic qualifier Kenyon Hill of Oklahoma, is a small, quiet buzzbait. It is a good lure that is particularly effective in calm conditions when the fish are suspended close to the surface in flat water.

"This little buzzer doesn't make much noise, so it's perfect around overhanging willows and situations like that," Hill claims. He believes the in-line buzzer is best suited for clear-water conditions as well as aquatic vegetation, because it tends to be more weedless than the safety pin style.

In contrast, the safety-pin type makes a great deal of noise. So this type of buzzer is used in situations where you need to call fish to the lure; situ-

ations like off-colored water and deeper water.

Hill is among many anglers who prefer to use the offset buzzer in dingy water, particularly around woody cover like brush, logs and boathouses.

"Over the years, I think the offset-type of buzzbait tends to produce more big bass than the in-line buzzer," adds Shaw Grigsby. "The offset buzzers are really state-of-the-art and you can do so many different things with them."

Mixing up the two styles of buzzers makes these baits more productive and extends their season. Start fishing buzzbaits in early spring and don't put them away until late in the fall.

In-Line Buzzer

Safety-Pin Buzzer

Buzzin' the weed tops is a dynamite bass-catching method.

provoke sensational strikes. In clear, rocky northern lakes, buzzbaits sometimes produce smallmouths over 6 pounds.

On a rippled surface – Most anglers believe that the water must be dead calm to fish a buzzbait, but a ripple on the surface usually enhances your success with the bait. And don't hesitate to try a buzzbait in rough water. Fish it over submerged weed beds or woody cover in shallow areas and, if possible, cast it into the wind and retrieve in the direction the wind is blowing.

In the rain – A buzzbait is a very noisy lure that is easily visible despite the surface disturbance caused by raindrops. But a buzzbait will work under sunny skies, as well. When it's sunny, you can see submerged objects more clearly, making it easier to target your casts. Plus, bass tend to hold tighter to these objects under sunny conditions, so their location is more predictable.

In streams – A buzzbait is a very good, but often overlooked, stream lure. Wade within casting distance of a submerged rock or log and run a buzzer over the top – you'll find out quickly whether or not a bass is there.

How to Fish a Buzzbait

To improve your odds of tangling with a big bass, you must vary your buzzbait presentation according to existing conditions. Besides the basic retrieve shown on page 126, here are some other retrieves to try:

Erratic retrieve – This is exactly the same as the basic retrieve, but when the lure is churning across the surface, occasionally turn the reel handle quickly to make the lure speed up in short, erratic bursts. This retrieve may trigger strikes from finicky bass.

Buzz-pole retrieve – This time-proven technique gives you thorough coverage of areas that would be difficult to reach by casting.

Rig up a long "buzz pole" or a cane pole with a piece of 30- to 50-pound mono the same length as the pole, then tie on an in-line buzzer. Most old-timers who use this technique add a big pork frog to help float the lure higher and give it more bulk.

Moving quietly through shallow areas, work the buzzer back and forth repeatedly across the surface, targeting isolated stumps. If you hook a bass and it swims back down into the cover and gets tangled, reach in with your hands to free it. Don't try to pull the fish out with the pole or you'll rip out the hook.

Bass often strike at a buzzbait and miss it. When this happens, many anglers immedi-ately reach for a "fallback lure" which they have pre-rigged on a separate rod that they keep close at hand and ready for instant use.

Captain Ray's favorite fallback lures include soft jerkbaits, leadhead grubs and plastic worms or lizards. He's had good suc-cess chunking a giant plastic worm into the exact spot where a big bass just missed his buzzbait. This is a great lunker technique when buzzin' isolated patches of milfoil or hydrilla. Usually, after slapping at the buzzbait, the bass stays in the immediate area and will instantly engulf a slow-sinking lure cast to the precise spot.

Polarized sunglasses are a must when fishing a buzzbait. They help you locate iso-lated stumps, brush piles and weed beds where big bass lurk. Watch carefully for tell-tale dark shadows revealing the presence of these fish-attracting objects.

A buzzbait may not be the most versatile bass lure, but in the right places, it's undoubtedly one of the most effective.

Recommended Tackle

A long baitcast-ing rod is pre-ferred for most buzzbait fishing. It shouldn't be overly stiff; a 6¹/₂- or 7-foot medium-action stick often works best. Stiff rods cause you to miss a lot of strikes, because you react too quickly and pull the bait out of the fish's mouth. A softer rod allows the fish to inhale the lure more deeply before you can react.

The rod should be paired with a heavy-duty bait-casting reel and 14- to 30-pound. abrasion-resistant mono.

Periodically speeding up your retrieve and kicking up a little extra spray helps trigger strikes.

The Basic Buzzbait Retrieve

Stand up so you can see submerged stumps, weed beds and other below-water cover.

Cast the buzzbait well past the target area and turn the reel handle to engage the spool just before the lure hits the water.

Hold the rod high (11 o'clock) and reel just fast enough to keep the lure churning across the surface.

Gradually lower the rod tip as the lure approaches the boat. If you keep your rod tip high, you'll pull the nose of the lure out of the water and the blade won't spin properly.

If a bass strikes and the lure disappears, lower the tip to 9 o'clock, hesitate a second or two and then set the hook as hard as you can.

If the bass misses the lure, continue reeling while pulling the lure to one side or the other. This will make the lure change direction suddenly, which often prompts a repeat strike.

Tips for Fishing Buzzbaits

Disassemble two identical tandem buzzers and remove the counter-rotating blades, which make the baits run straight. Reassemble the baits so that each one has identical blades. This way, one of the baits will veer to the right; the other, to the left.

Select the buzzer that veers in the direction of hard-to-reach cover, like the shadowed area under a dock. Cast parallel to the cover; when you retrieve, the bait will veer into the fish zone.

Bend the arm of a safety-pin buzzer to make the blade just barely tick the shaft as it spins. The extra noise often makes a big difference.

Cast a buzzer into the shadowed area beneath trees growing along shore. Bass in shady areas are more likely to hit a surface lure.

The Facts of Froggin'

by Tim Tucker

From the time that early man first attempted to copy nature by carving wooden objects into forms that would fool gamefish, fishermen have always had a special affection for the topwater frog.

Surface-fished frogs have evolved from their earliest and crudest forms (for which collectors now pay top dollar) to today's realistic amphibians, but all have shared a special place among fishermen, most notably bass fishermen. The allure of using this natural-prey imitation to fool large-mouth bass has not wavered through the years.

Lure-collecting historian R. Stephen Irwin, M.D., ranks topwater frogs third in terms of antiquity. The first imitation frog, the Kent Champion Floater, was born in 1880. A decade later, James Heddon, father of artificial lure-making, began hand-carving surface frogs for his own use. In 1906, Shakespeare marketed the Rhodes Mechanical Swimming Frog, a patented surface lure that featured legs that seemed to kick as the bait was pulled through the water.

Heddon was encouraged by Dr. James Henshall (author of the first book about the black bass), to introduce a line of wooden frog-like baits, beginning with the Luny Frog in 1927.

The day of the wooden frog is over, but not, apparently, the heyday of the surface frog. The popularity of topwater frogs is evident in the role reserved for these lures by fishermen throughout the country, including those on the highly competitive professional tournament trails.

Frogs are an underrated food source for bass, claims renowned big-bass authority Doug Hannon. "In my thousands of hours of documenting big-bass behavior, both on and under the water, I've observed bass eating frogs countless times", he says. "And the biggest bass – the lunkers – get big by feeding on prey that is easily caught – like frogs."

That explains the allure of topwater frogs for both fish and fishermen.

Know Your Frogs

All of the frog-like lures made today are constructed from rubber or plastic, in varying degrees of hardness. But a wide range of models exist, including some lures that vaguely resemble a frog because of their bulky form and others so lifelike that they could end up on the fork of a gig.

The most popular surface frogs used today are the soft-rubber weedless floaters, like the Snagproof Frog, Bill Plummer Superfrog, Renosky Natural Frog and Harrison-Hoge Super Frog. All are made of a very pliable rubber and feature limber, almost lifelike legs that shake and quiver when pulled through the water, slightly resembling the kicking action of a real frog.

But, generally, frog-imitating lures have very little built-in action; it has to be created by rhythmically moving the rod tip. These types of topwater frogs are largely weedless through the use of a wire weedguard or the positioning of the hooks, which point upward from the rear of the bait.

There are other types of soft rubber or plastic frogs like the Mister Twister Hawg Frawg, which come without hooks and are usually rigged Texas-style with a regular worm hook.

Popular Surface Frogs

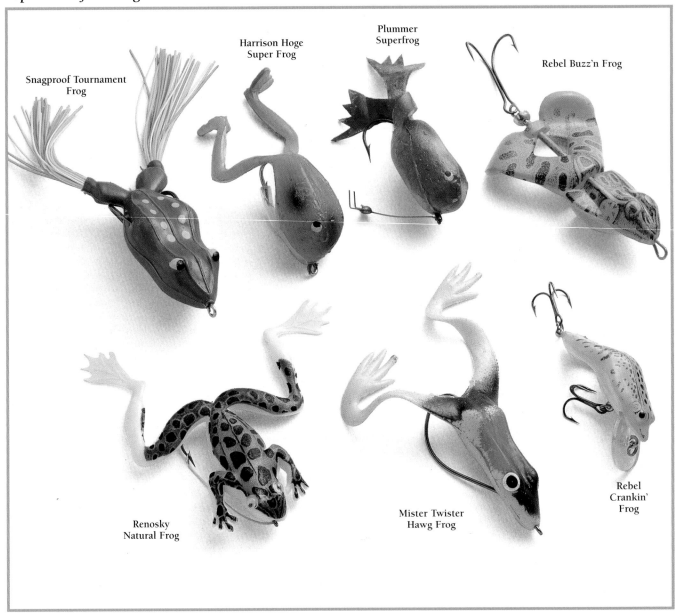

Snagproof Tournament Frog

Harrison Hoge Super Frog

Plummer Superfrog

Rebel Buzz'n Frog

Renosky Natural Frog

Mister Twister Hawg Frog

Rebel Crankin' Frog

Although it specializes in hard-plastic lures, Rebel has some frog-like baits that have developed quite a following.

The Rebel Wee-Frog is an ultralight crankbait that dives as deep as 3 feet, but can be fished effectively on the surface as well. When sitting still in the water, this floater/diver is submerged, except for its protruding eyes that peek out of the water, much like they eyes of a real frog resting on the water. The Wee-Frog line includes several realistic color patterns for each season.

The Rebel Buzz'n Frog is a larger bait with natural color patterns that assumes the same profile when sitting quietly in the water. But begin retrieving it and it suddenly acts like a buzzbait. Its legs are molded into a diamond shape and spin, creating a buzzbait-like disturbance on the surface. With its unique twin hooks (which point upward), the Buzz'n Frog is largely weedless and can be fished in the same places you would normally use a buzzbait.

Froggin' Tips from the Pros

"I find myself using rubber frogs more and more these days," says all-time tournament king Roland Martin. "It's one of the standard baits now, just like a Johnson

Basic Types of Surface Frogs

Soft-rubber weedless floaters have lifelike legs that produce a realistic kicking action when you retrieve with short twitches.

A Texas-rigged soft-plastic frog is the most weedless type of frog imitation.

Crankbait-type frogs can be used as subsurface baits as well as topwaters.

Buzzin' frogs create more surface disturbance than other types, often drawing dramatic topwater strikes.

Roland Martin and a frog-caught bass.

rushes and reeds – an unlikely application for these baits, it would seem.

Martin fishes the Bill Plummer Superfrog and Snagproof Frog in a variety of situations that stretch from spring through fall. It is a surprisingly effective lure for spawning bass, he claims.

"Any time you have spawning fish, many of them are going to be in almost inaccessible places," Martin explains. "On Lake Okeechobee, some fish will spawn in places so thick that you have to use totally weedless baits.

"A topwater plug is out of the question. Bedding bass love to hit a topwater bait, but you just can't fish it in that situation. But you can fish a weedless frog and, unlike a spoon, you can stop it and twitch it without it sinking to the bottom. These frogs are strictly a topwater lure and can even be fished in open pockets, just like a Devil's Horse or Rapala. And it's the only completely weedless topwater there is."

Summertime brings good surface fishing and Martin spends a considerable amount of time "frogging the pads," as he calls it. He concentrates on large lily pad fields, where bass seek the extra shade, added oxygen and cooler water that the pads provide.

Martin fishes the surface frog slowly, allowing it to linger when pulled up on a pad or dropped into a small open-water pocket.

One of former Red Man All-American champion Joe Thomas' most dependable secret weapons on the national tournament circuit is a surface-popping version of a soft-plastic frog that is like nothing else on the market. The Snagproof Tournament Popper features a large, flat face that displaces water, lively silicone legs, internal rattles and strong round-bend hooks.

"It has several advantages over other similar baits," the Ohio pro claims. "It's injection molded where a lot of them are not, so it's very durable and will last a long time.

Joe Thomas.

spoon. A Johnson spoon should to be in everybody's tackle box. A guy is crazy not to keep one in his box. And a guy is crazy not to have a weedless frog in his box if he is serious about his bass fishing."

Frog-like lures were designed for fishing vegetation and little else. The most common applications for these weedless baits are lily pads, moss and dense vegetation that has peaked out and matted on the surface. But Martin has also had good success fishing surface frogs in vertical vegetation like bul-

And they've taken great pains to make a bait that is ready to fish out of the package. We no longer have to modify the baits by putting bigger hooks in them, adding skirts, cutting the legs off and other things."

Unlike other topwater frogs, the Tournament Popper dives several inches below the surface with a strong jerk of the rod. "I get a lot of strikes as soon as the bait breaks back to the surface," Thomas says.

"This bait is great for lily pads and any type of matted vegetation, like hydrilla and milfoil, that forms a canopy in 5 feet or less of water," he explains. "While other frogs make noise to some degree, this popper and its chugging sound will pull in fish from way below the surface mat."

Guido Hibdon.

When the milfoil or hydrilla reaches peak density on lakes like Missouri's Lake of the Ozarks or Sam Rayburn Reservoir in Texas, former BASS Masters Classic champion Guido Hibdon sharpens the hooks on his rubber frogs and begins randomly retrieving them over the vegetation. The weeds are so thick they will support the weight of the frog, and the bass can detect its vibration as it moves overhead.

The bass usually take the bait in one of two ways: blow up through the grass to inhale the fake frog or wait for it to fall into an open hole or pockets in the vegetation before grabbing it.

"From July through September, the moss gets so thick that we take the boat and run through it to tear it up and create some holes," says Hibdon, a long-time guide and tournament pro from Gravois Mills, Missouri. "I can't tell you how many times I have done that and gone back the next day with that frog and caught bass from the holes we made the day before."

Most frog-fishing experts believe that lure color isn't much of a factor. Bass lurking below a surface mat see only a dark silhouette moving across the grass. That may be the reason that the majority of manufacturers stick to basic colors – white, black, brown, green and yellow. Hibdon, however, scores most consistently with the leopard frog color pattern.

The thick vegetation sometimes makes it a challenge to set the hook effectively and then pull the bass – particularly a big bass – from the weeds. In fact, Hibdon usually doesn't even attempt to pull the fish free. Instead, he sets the hook as well as he can and, while keeping a taut line, goes to the fish, where a little gardening is in order. He actually pulls the grass off of the bass until he can get a firm grip on it.

According to Hibdon, the most common mistake in fishing frogs is setting the hook too soon. It takes nerves of steel to be able to watch a bass blast though the vegetation and nail the frog while resisting the urge to set the hook.

Recommended Tackle

Frog fishing demands heavy tackle. Most pros combine a 7½-foot flipping stick and a baitcasting reel spooled with 20- to 30-pound-test line, either abrasion-resistant mono or super-line. The long, stout rod serves three important purposes: making long casts, setting the hook from a distance and horsing the fish out of lily pads or other dense weeds.

Frog fishing generally takes place in expanses of shallow vegetation where the strike zone can be enormous, so making long casts and working the bait all the way back to the boat is crucial.

Snagproof Tournament Popper

How to Fish a Weedless Frog

Toss the bait into openings in the vegetation and hesitate long enough for the ripples to subside. Or, cast the bait right onto the weed mat.

Skitter the bait across the weeds, hesitating whenever it comes to an open spot.

When you see a boil, hesitate until you feel the weight of the fish before setting the hook.

Apply steady upward pressure to keep the fish's head out of the weeds and prevent it from diving and tangling your line.

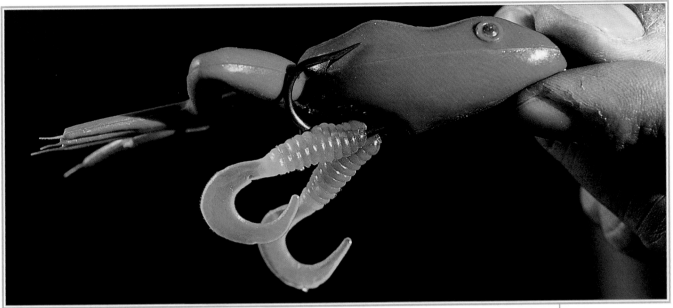

Add small (1") curly tail grubs to your frog for extra attraction. Hook one grub on each of the hooks. The grubs give the bait considerably more action than the rubber legs alone.

Four Froggin' Tips

Frogs are known to be "bum hookers," but you can significantly improve your hooking percentage by bending the hooks slightly outward.

Cut a small hole in the frog's body and add BBs. The shot makes a subtle sound that seems to attract bass, and the extra weight helps in casting.

Add a 6- to 12-inch leader to one of the hooks and tie on a small plastic worm or tube jig. If a bass misses the bait, hesitate and allow the worm or tube to sink; the bass will usually take it.

Make a tandem frog rig by tying on a pair of frogs spaced about 3 feet apart. Should a bass miss the front lure, it will often attack the second one.

Propbait Principles

by Mark Hicks

Funny thing about propbaits: they were tagging largemouths long before any of today's bass pros were born, and they're as effective today as ever. Yet, propbaits' popularity has slipped greatly as modern anglers are filling their tackle boxes with the newest "hot" lures.

Ironically, bass in most waters now see a barrage of the latest spinnerbaits, crankbaits, jigs and soft plastics, but they rarely see a propbait. Recognizing this phenomenon, some of the top bass pros are spending more time tossing these sputtering topwaters.

In case you're not familiar with propbaits, they have a cigar-shaped body sporting metal propellers fore and aft, and two or three treble hooks. This simple design has withstood the test of time. Many propbaits are still carved from wood, while others are fabricated from plastic. Excellent models are available in both materials.

Propellers are what set propbaits apart from other topwater lures. The metal blades come in various styles and sizes, but they all perform the same primary function— making noise that attracts bass!

There is little doubt that bass mistake propbaits for baitfish, and no question that the clamoring blades are a major part of this illusion. Subtle retrieves may emulate a shad slapping the water. When twitched aggressively, some propbaits mimic the sound of a bass ripping a baitfish from the surface.

This no doubt arouses a competitive instinct and bass come quickly to share in the feast or take advantage of crippled prey. Many anglers contend that the uproar caused by a propbait aggravates bass into action or arouses their curiosity.

One angler who has not forgotten about the power of propbaits is John Hunt, a Tennessean whose ability to catch bass on Kentucky and Barkley lakes is nothing short of legendary. Hunt is the proprietor of Hunt's Outdoors, a sporting goods store located in Waverly, Tennessee, about 10 miles east of Kentucky Lake. While Hunt is noted for beguiling bass with crankbaits, few anglers are aware that a propbait called a "Jumper" has accounted for a number of his heavy catches.

When & Where to Fish Propbaits

"Propbaits catch fish year around," says Hunt. "I primarily use them in fall, because the water gets clearer then. Any topwater bait works better in clear water."

Another factor that makes propbaits so effective in fall is the increased baitfish activity that occurs at this time, especially with shad. As the weather cools, schools of shad migrate into creek arms. They suspend at various depths and can often be seen rippling the water. The ever-moving clusters appear as dark, swirling clouds just under the surface.

Bass follow their forage and grow more accustomed to feeding near the surface. As the water cools and daylight diminishes, bass are more inclined to strike topwater offerings throughout the day.

John Hunt

John Hunt is not a full-time professional bass fisherman, but his credentials read like one. He has long been a dominating angler on Kentucky and Barkley lakes, has qualified for the BASS Masters Classic via the club route, has earned berths in Red Man All-Americans and won a U.S. Bass tournament worth $110,000 on Sam Rayburn Reservoir.

Hunt lives and works in Waverly, Tennessee, where he is the owner and operator of Hunt's Outdoors.

"The prime time," says Hunt, "is when reservoirs are pulled down to winter pool. Say you've got a creek channel with 10 to 20 feet of water that winds through a shallow flat. Look for stumps on the edge of the channel in 2 to 5 feet. That's where you'll find those big old bass feeding up for wintertime."

Hunt and a friend took advantage of this pattern a few years ago during a warm spell in mid-December. With only an afternoon to fish, they blitzed shallow, stumpy points with spinnerbaits, crankbaits and other lures without getting a strike.

Past experiences nagged at Hunt. The water had warmed up to 60° F. He knew the bass just had to be there. He and his friend tied on propbaits and made another run at the stumps. "In the next hour and a half," he recalls, "we caught 10 bass that weighed over 60 pounds. They just ate up our baits. It was one of those dream days."

Rippling water caused by shad activity is a signal to try propbaits.

Propbaits can also be effective in spring, when bass move shallow and are preoccupied with spawning. Then, they must be fished with a slow, quiet retrieve.

You can't go wrong fishing propbaits around stumps and other visible bass hideouts, such as fallen trees, standing timber, weed edges, boat docks and rocky points. Cast beyond likely objects when possible. Work the propbait close and stall it within easy range of any bass that may be using the cover. Take a deep breath to calm your nerves and let the bass stew. Chances are that the next nudge will ignite a watery explosion.

Selecting Propbaits

Most propbaits have a long, thin body that is pointed on both ends. These baits slide through the water easily, producing a subtle action that works well in most situations. Models with propellers on both ends

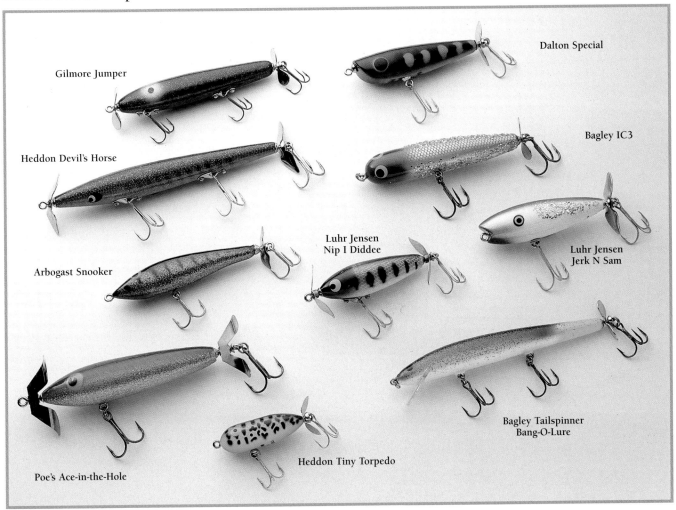

Gilmore Jumper

Dalton Special

Heddon Devil's Horse

Bagley IC3

Arbogast Snooker

Luhr Jensen
Nip I Diddee

Luhr Jensen
Jerk N Sam

Poe's Ace-in-the-Hole

Heddon Tiny Torpedo

Bagley Tailspinner
Bang-O-Lure

create more surface disturbance than those with only a single propeller. A few propbaits have a flattened or cupped face, which results in a more erratic action.

Size of the lure and its blades also affect how the lure responds. Probaits generally come in $3/8$, $1/2$, $5/8$ and $3/4$-ounce sizes. Larger baits with bigger props generate a more noticeable fracas. They would be a good choice when bass are aggressive, feeding on large baitfish, holding deep or when the water is choppy.

Smaller, quieter baits generally draw more strikes when you're confronted with calm conditions, shallow water and bass that are more reserved. For an even more toned-down presentation, select a propbait with a propellers only on the tail.

Hunt favors dark colors in most situations. In fact, his favorite propbait, nick-named "Old Blue," is a dark blue "Jumper"

(above). He believes dark blue colors silhouette nicely against the sky during low light conditions early and late in the day, when propbaits are generally more productive. He also believes that a dark color is more visible to bass in the stained water common in riverine reservoirs like Kentucky and Barkley lakes.

When fishing clear water under sunny conditions, Hunt switches to a lighter color, such as white and blue.

How to Fish a Propbait

Consistent success with propbaits requires that you match the lure's action to the mood of the bass. A good starting point would be a cadence of several moderate twitches followed by a pause. Hunt often pulls a propbait ahead 6 to 8 inches at a time with a Juke, Juke, Juke-Juke; Juke, Juke, Juke-Juke.

A medium-power, medium-action baitcasting rod will do a nice job of imparting action to most propbaits. Your reel should be capable of making long casts with fairly heavily line, say 14- or 17-pound mono. The heavy line is necessary to keep the bait waltzing on the surface. Thinner lines tend to sink and pull the nose of these lures under.

If that doesn't work, he may try shorter twitches with longer pauses or a more aggressive action that really sputters the surface. You'll know you've found the right combination when a bass explodes on the bait.

In spring, when bass are in spawning mode, an even better recourse would be a floating minnowbait with a tailspinner. Floating minnowbaits have always been deadly in spring. These lures entice bass with proven minnow bodies that have the additional sass, splash and flash of tail props.

Accurate casting is important in propbait fishing, especially when hard shadows or currents cause bass to hold tight to stumps, logs and similar objects. This is when you should concentrate on working propbaits within about 6 inches of the cover.

Pinpoint casting is also a must when chucking a propbait into holes in weed beds that have grown to the surface. This is common with hydrilla, milfoil and similar forms of aquatic vegetation. If you can consistently pitch a propbait to the backside of a 3-foot diameter pothole and dance it across the opening, you're going to receive many rude interruptions from sizable largemouth bass.

Casting accuracy isn't nearly as crucial when fishing propbaits over subsurface structures, such as points and submergent weed beds. Accuracy is even less important when bass are suspended beneath schools of shad in open water or hovering over ledges and other structures that drop into deeper water. Casting distance, however, is critical in these situations.

In clear water, bass may come up from depths of 20 feet to blast one of these lures. You need to stay back and make long casts to avoid spooking the fish. Thankfully, most propbaits work well for distance casting.

Propbaits won't replace your other basic bass lures. But when the time is right, they'll produce more strikes and excitement than anything else you can throw.

Casting accuracy is important for placing the bait into likely fish-holding cover.

How to Tune a Propbait

If the blades are not spinning properly, bend them to change the angle and, if necessary, twist them to adjust the pitch.

Test the blades to make sure they spin easily by blowing on them or by holding the bait out the window of a moving car.

Few propbaits are rigged with propellers that are sturdy enough to withstand much abuse. Brawl with a big bass or bounce one of these lures off a hard object and a blade is likely to bend out of kilter.

Some blades are thin and supple and you can easily twist them back into place with your fingers. Others are stiff and require judicious work with needle-nose pliers.

Before beginning, be sure you understand what you're trying to accomplish. Ideally, you took time to study the blades before fishing with the lure. If not, hopefully you have a

backup to use as a reference. With double-bladed propbaits, usually only one blade at a time becomes dysfunctional. The other blade may be used as a model.

Note that each end of the prop has an opposing pitch that makes it spin when pulled through the water. A flatter pitch creates more resistance and noise, while a deeper pitch makes the blade spin faster with less resistance. With many propbaits, you can alter the pitch to achieve the action you desire.

Tips for Fishing Propbaits

Twitch a propbait on a slack line to achieve a sharper popping action (inset). Also, a slack-line pop moves the bait only a few inches, enabling you to keep it over good cover longer than you otherwise could.

Use a tail-weighted propbait for a side-to-side, "walk-the-dog" action (inset). With the tail riding deeper, the head of the bait swings to the side more easily, resulting in the erratic action that active bass often prefer.

LIVE BAIT

Live Bait to the Rescue

by Dick Sternberg

The practice of using live bait for bass is on the decline in many areas, primarily because anglers have become increasingly proficient with artificial lures.

But the fact remains that nothing is as effective at convincing a stubborn bass to bite than real food. This explains why anglers faced with tough conditions still turn to live bait to save the day.

For example, in California's ultra-clear big-bass reservoirs, where heavy recreational traffic and angling pressure make the fish super-finicky, savvy anglers know that they can fool a few of the giant bass with live crayfish.

In Florida's famed trophy bass lakes, the majority of the 10-plus pounders taken each year are pulled off the spawning beds using giant golden shiners. Though this method is highly controversial, there is no argument about its effectiveness.

Not only is live-bait fishing one of the best ways to catch a real trophy, it may be the only way to catch bass under extremely adverse conditions. After a severe cold front, for instance, experienced guides know they can still catch a few bass by dangling live bait in their face. Live bait can even draw bites when the water temperature is near freezing and the fish are turning up their noses at artificials.

Because bass have such a highly varied diet, the list of live baits that can be used is virtually endless. Effective baits range in size from inch-long crickets to foot-long shiners.

Live bait is more commonly used in fishing for smallmouth bass, spotted bass and stripers than it is for largemouth bass. Leeches and nightcrawlers, for instance, are favorite smallmouth baits in many of the northern states and Canada. Spring lizards are a traditional bait for smallmouth and spotted bass throughout the Southeast. And

large shad are considered the premier bait for big stripers in reservoirs and rivers from coast to coast.

Another reason for the declining popularity of live bait is the difficulty of obtaining the right bait and then caring for it so it stays in good condition.

Few anglers are lucky enough to live near a good bait shop with a dependable supply of the type of bait they need. They either must travel a long distance to find the right bait or learn to catch their own. We'll give you some tips for catching your own bait and keeping it alive.

Some baits, like gizzard shad, are rarely sold in bait shops because they are nearly impossible to keep alive for more than a day or two. Consequently, anglers intent on using these baits must learn how to catch and care for their own.

Other baits, such as golden shiners, may be sold at bait shops, but bass experts know that the store-bought baits won't produce like the wild ones. Wild golden shiners have a natural fear of bass. When a bass approaches, a hooked shiner swims excitedly in an attempt to escape, usually drawing an aggressive strike. A pond-reared shiner, on the other hand, has no fear of bass and struggles very little, so bass might tend to ignore it.

But even fresh, healthy live bait does not automatically guarantee success. On the pages that follow, NAFC Members will learn when to use various types of live bait, how to rig the bait properly and how to present it so it looks natural enough to fool the bass.

Frogs

When you think of live-bait fishing for bass, frogs are one of the first baits that come to mind. A few decades ago, frogs

This big smallmouth fell for a lively jumbo leech.

Bass can't resist the natural kicking action of a frog.

were commonly sold in bait shops and, in some areas, are still a popular bait. After all, what could be more tempting to a bass than a live frog kicking its way through shallow weeds?

The leopard frog is, by far, the most common bait species, although green frogs and pickerel frogs are sometimes used in the eastern half of the country.

Today, few bait shops carry frogs, so you'll have to catch your own. Luckily, that's not too difficult. Just walk along the marshy shore of a creek and nab them with a dip net or, if you're quick, by hand.

You can keep frogs in most any kind of container, as long as it breathes or has air holes. Preferably it should have an opening at the top that allows you to reach in to grab a frog without the others jumping out.

Keep your frogs at room temperature or a little cooler and out of direct sun. If you plan on keeping them for more than a few days, they'll need food and water. You can feed them crickets or other live insects.

Most anglers select frogs from 3 to 4 inches long. The rigging method depends mainly on the cover. For fishing shallow weeds, simply push a weedless hook through the lips. For deeper, clean-bottomed areas, use an open hook and add split-shot about a foot up the line, as needed.

The trick is to let the frog kick naturally, rather than pulling it along. Inch it in slowly,

Tips for Fishing with Frogs

Keep frogs in a wire-mesh box with a slitted rubber lid. This way, you can put frogs in and take them out without losing any.

Push a size 2 to 4 weedless hook through the frog's lips, as shown. You can use a weighted hook (foreground) or a weedless hook (background).

Live Bait to the Rescue

letting the frog do the work. If the frog starts to weaken and lose its kick, put on a new one.

When fishing in lily pads or other dense cover, be sure to use heavy line, at least 20-pound test.

Salamanders & Waterdogs

A good-size bass will take most any kind of salamander, but the ones most commonly used as bait are spring lizards and waterdogs.

Spring lizards include several species of "lungless" salamanders that are found along the edges of cold springs and brooks or in cool, moist wooded areas in the eastern half of the country. Four- to six-inchers make the best bait.

You can buy spring lizards in bait shops throughout the southeastern states. Or, you can catch your own after dark by donning a headlamp and picking them off rocks along the banks of small streams. Sometimes you can find them in window wells.

Refrigerate spring lizards in an ice cream bucket half filled with moist leaves or moss. Be sure to perforate the lid.

Small spring lizards are often used to tip a jig. Larger ones can be fished on a split-shot or slip-sinker rig.

A waterdog is the larval stage of the common tiger salamander. Easily identified by its external gills, tiny legs and long, unbroken

Waterdog.

fin that wraps around much of its body, the water-dog is a much better bait than the adult tiger salamander. Most anglers prefer 4- to 6-inchers, although trophy largemouth hunters sometimes use waterdogs up to 10 inches long.

Waterdogs are sporadically available in bait shops throughout the country. Some anglers seine their own in small ponds that usually dry up in summer.

Because waterdogs still have gills, you must keep them in water, preferably in a styrofoam container. Try to keep the water at about 50°F and change it weekly.

Waterdogs are rigged and fished in the same manner as spring lizards, although the hooking method differs slightly (below).

How to Hook Spring Lizards & Waterdogs

Push a size 2 to 4 bait hook through the tough skin ahead of a spring lizard's hind leg when fishing it on a split-shot or slip-sinker rig. To tip a jig, hook the bait through the lips.

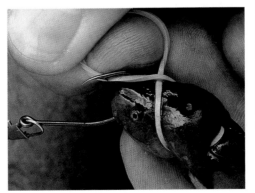
Secure a waterdog on a size 2 to 4 hook by looping a rubber band around the head and over the hook point as shown. Or, secure it with a plastic disc (p.87).

Golden shiner.

Golden Shiners

Big golden shiners have long been a top producer of giant largemouths, particularly in Florida's natural lakes. But California anglers are finding that shiners work equally well for extracting huge bass from Golden State impoundments.

Golden shiners are available in bait shops throughout the country, but real trophy hounds prefer catching their own wild shiners, for reasons previously mentioned. Shiners used for big largemouths range in length from 8 to 12 inches.

If you know of a lake that holds big golden shiners, chum a shallow, weedy area with oatmeal. When the shiners start dimpling the surface, try fishing for them using a tiny piece of dampened bread molded onto a size 12 hook, or throw a cast net over the school.

Shiners are difficult to keep alive in warm weather, so they're used most extensively during the cool-water months. Even then, you must keep them well aerated and avoid overcrowding.

In Florida, shiners are normally fished on a weedless hook beneath a float and lobbed into openings in shallow weedbeds. This approach requires a 7½- to 8½-foot, heavy-power baitcasting rod and 30- to 40-pound line to horse hooked bass out of the cover.

When a bass approaches a wild golden shiner, the baitfish may become so frantic that it skitters on the surface. When this happens, get ready; a bite is only seconds away.

Another good shallow-water technique, especially around matted weeds, is freelining. Hook the shiner through the tail with no extra weight and let it pull your line under the dense surface mat. You can also freeline in shallow water with only sparse weed growth

For fishing deeper, cleaner-bottomed water, such as California impoundments, you can get by with a 6-foot, medium-heavy-power spinning rod with 8- or 10-pound mono. With an open hook and a ¼-ounce

How to Rig Golden Shiners

Peg a cylindrical float onto your line and then hook a golden shiner through the lips as shown, using a weedless shiner hook in sizes 2/0 to 4/0.

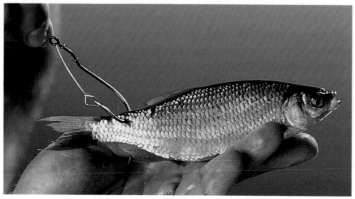

For freelining, hook the shiner in the tail, using a size 2/0 to 4/0 weedless shiner hook or, if the cover is light, a size 1/0 to 3/0 open hook.

Live Bait to the Rescue

weight about 18 inches up the line, you can fish the bait as deep as 45 feet.

Shad

Although shad are the predominant bait-fish in many of the country's top bass lakes, they are seldom used to catch largemouth or smallmouth. But they have gained a reputation as one of the most reliable baits for trophy stripers.

The species most often used as bait is the gizzard shad. The threadfin shad is smaller and not as hardy. You can easily tell the difference by looking at the tail. On the gizzard shad, it has a blackish margin; on the threadfin, yellowish. For stripers of 20 pounds or more, use shad from 10 to 15 inches in length.

Shad are even more difficult to keep alive than golden shiners, so you'll rarely find them in bait shops. Most anglers go out in the morning and use a cast net to catch enough shad for a day of fishing. They keep the shad in large, insulated, aerated tanks.

Many striper guides rely on a technique called balloon fishing. Using a heavy flippin' stick and 20-pound mono, fish the shad, unweighted, beneath a partially-inflated party balloon tied around the line with a single overhand knot. Shad are strong swimmers and will tow the bait in circles around the boat. The more line you let out, the more area the shad will cover.

A balloon works much better than on ordinary float, because its buoyancy keeps it on top of the water, so there is practically no drag to slow down and wear out the shad. When

Gizzard shad.

How to Rig Live Shad

For balloon fishing, push a size 3/0 to 6/0 hook through the back, just in front of the dorsal fin. Tie a balloon around the line with an overhand knot (inset).

For trolling, push the hook through the nostrils, as shown. Hooked this way, the shad will stay lively, and the nostrils are much tougher than the lips.

Ribbon leech.

How to Rig Leeches

For slip-sinker or split-shot fishing, push a size 6 hook through the leech, just above the sucker. When nibbling panfish are a problem, hook the leech through the tougher neck area (opposite end).

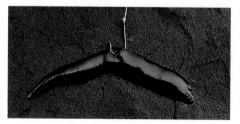

For slip-bobber fishing, hook the leech through the middle, using a size 6 hook or a 1/32-ounce jighead. This way, the leech keeps swimming even when the rig is not moving.

a striper grabs the bait, you'll see the balloon bouncing as the line slides through the overhand knot. If the striper makes a fast run, the balloon usually pops.

Some striper guides prefer trolling with live shad, because they can cover much more area. You can troll the shad on a flat line or add sinkers to get the bait down as much as 40 feet. Some anglers even troll live shad on downriggers or side planers. Whatever technique you use, troll very slowly (less than 1 mph) for a natural presentation.

Leeches

Smallmouth guides in the northern states know that smallies love leeches. In fact, when leeches first became popular in the late 1960s, guides used them to make eye-popping smallmouth catches in lakes that were thought be "fished out."

The ribbon leech (*Nephelopsis obscura*) is, by far, the most popular bait leech. Surprisingly, it is seldom found in the lakes with good populations of smallmouth or other game fish. It abounds in shallow, marshy "duck" lakes.

Leeches are widely available in bait shops, but you can easily catch your own by placing a fresh fish head in a coffee can along with a few rocks to hold it down. Pinch the top of the can, leaving just enough room for leeches to get in, then set it in the shallows around the fringe of a marsh known to hold leeches. Pick it up the next morning and remove the leeches.

Some anglers prefer "jumbo" leeches, which measure up to 6 inches long when swimming. But smallmouth aren't fussy; they'll hit a leech of practically any size as long as it's lively.

The secret to keeping leeches healthy is cold water. If the water they're in is allowed to exceed 50°F, adult leeches start to spawn and will die within a few days. In warm weather, keep them in an insulated container, such as a styrofoam bucket or small cooler, and add ice as needed. For long-term storage, keep them refrigerated at a temperature of 40 degrees or less and change water every few days.

A medium-power spinning outfit with 6- to 8-pound mono is ideal for leech fishing. You can work depths of 15 to 30 feet using a slip-sinker rig with a ¼- to ⅜-ounce weight. For casting into shallow water, simply add a split shot or two about 18 inches above the hook. You can also use a small leech to tip a jig.

Perhaps the deadliest smallmouth technique of all, especially when you know right where the fish are, is dangling a leech beneath a slip-bobber. Even when smallmouths or, for that matter, largemouths, are off the bite, they find it hard to resist a lively leech wiggling in their face.

Nightcrawlers

Nightcrawlers and leeches can be used interchangeably for any kind of black bass, the main difference being that crawlers are not as tough and are easily nipped off by panfish.

Nightcrawlers are available at practically any bait shop and kids commonly sell them at roadside stands. But many anglers prefer to collect their own by going out with a flashlight on a rainy night. In only an hour or two, you can pick enough worms from a well-established lawn or golf course to last the entire season.

Six- to eight-inch crawlers are adequate for most bass fishing. Bass will hit the foot-long "snakes," but you'll lose a lot more fish.

Like leeches, crawlers require cool temperatures. Keep your stock refrigerated in worm bedding and, for a day of fishing, bring only as many worms as you need and keep them in a small container in a cooler with plenty of ice.

The techniques for fishing crawlers are pretty much the same as those used for leeches. You can fish them on a slip-sinker or split-shot rig, or dangle them beneath a slip-bobber. And a ⅛-ounce jighead tipped with half a crawler is one of the best-ever smallmouth baits.

Crayfish

Crayfish are a significant food item in the diet of all black bass, but they're especially important to smallmouth, probably because both share the same rocky habitat.

Only a few decades ago, crayfish were considered the premier live bait for smallmouth

Nightcrawler.

How to Rig Nightcrawlers

For slip-sinker or split-shot fishing, push a size 4 short-shank hook into the very tip of the worm's head, then run the point out the side about ¼ inch down. Hooked this way, the worm will trail straight.

To tip a jig, pinch the worm in half, then thread the end onto the hook. The head end seems to work a little better than the tail, although bass will hit either.

Crayfish

few states, however, the sale of crayfish has been banned in an effort to stop the spread of non-indigenous crayfish species.

To catch your own, simply wade a shallow, rocky stream, turning over large, flat rocks and intercepting crayfish with a dip net as they attempt to scoot away. Or, if you need a lot of crayfish, try seining them out of a shallow pond.

You can keep crayfish for weeks by placing them between layers of wet newspaper in a cooler and refrigerating them. For a day of fishing, pack crayfish in damp weeds or moss and keep them cool.

bass and, in some regions, they still are. Although used much less for largemouth, they are an extremely popular trophy largemouth bait in the big-bass lakes of southern California.

There are dozens of species of freshwater crayfish but, when it comes to selecting bait, species is much less important than size. Most bass anglers prefer 3 to 4 inches; larger ones result in too many missed bites. Softshell crayfish, those that have recently completed molting, seem to work a little better than hardshells.

In areas where they are popular, crayfish can be purchased at most bait shops. In a

The most effective way to present a crayfish is "stitching" it very slowly along the bottom. Using a sensitive spinning rod and 6- to 8-pound mono, lob-cast the bait, let it sink to the bottom and pull the line in very slowly with your hand. When a few feet of slack accumulates, reel it up, then stitch in some more. One retrieve may take five minutes. When you feel a take, tighten up the line until you feel resistance and set the hook. Bass inhale the bait, so there is no need to wait.

Other Bass Baits

Ask bass fishermen in different parts of the country to name their favorite live baits,

How to Rig Crayfish

Push a size 4 or 6 short-shank hook through the bony "horn" on the head. Hooked this way, the crayfish is not likely to scoot backward and crawl under a rock.

For depths of 10 feet or less, fish the bait unweighted or, if needed, add a round split shot (shown). For deeper water, use a Baitwalker rig to minimize snagging.

and you'll wind up with a list as long as your arm. Stream smallmouth fishermen in Ohio will tell you that nothing can compare to a live hellgrammite (dobson fly larva). In many northern states, shiner minnows, particularly spottail shiners, get the nod for smallmouth. In parts of the deep South, the siren (a giant salamander with no hind legs) is considered a top bait for largemouth. Along the Atlantic Coast, many striper fishermen swear by American eels up to 18 inches in length. Some anglers catch bass on crickets, grasshoppers and various other insect baits in both adult and larval forms.

To keep a hellgrammite alive, slip a size 4 or 6 hook under the collar (top). Threading it on a long-shank hook (bottom) will kill it.

Four Tips for selecting Good Bait

Look for minnows that school tightly in the corner of the bait tank or hang near the bottom. If the minnows are scattered all over the tank and swimming listlessly, they're not healthy.

Inspect leeches closely; if you see white fungus growing on any of them, or if they feel soft and squishy, don't buy them.

Check a box of crawlers before purchasing them. If you find a dead one, if most of them are too small or if they look stringy and weak instead of fat and lively, buy your bait elsewhere.

Don't buy medium leeches (top) or horse leeches (bottom). These leeches have a soft texture and are much less active in the hand than ribbon leeches.

Index

Z